There's Nothing
Like a Breast

There's Nothing Like a Breast

Diane Craig Chechik

Library of Congress Catalog Card Number: 99-90873
ISBN 0-9620549-1-7

Photograph permission by Ocean Images (UK), Ltd.
Cover Design: Mark Ray, St. Louis, Missouri
Editor: Laurie Rosin

CATALYST PUBLISHING, INC.
P. O. Box 20572
Sarasota, Florida 34276-3572
Email: dpcc12@aol.com
www.breast-cancer-survivor.com

CONTENTS

Foreword xiii

Prologue xxvii

Chapter 1 1

Chapter 2 11

Chapter 3 17

Chapter 4 23

Chapter 5 29

Chapter 6 41

Chapter 7 49

Chapter 8 55

Chapter 9 63

Chapter 10 71

Chapter 11 79

Chapter 12 87

Chapter 13 95

Chapter 14 105

Chapter 15 113

Chapter 16 119

Chapter 17 125

Epilogue 131

ACKNOWLEDGMENTS

My success with my book *There's Nothing Like a Breast* is greatly due to the astute, delicate, and fine editing of Laurie Rosin. Marc David Chechik's and Joel Craig Chechik's constant support is always with me, as well as is that of John Royle and Trudie Martineau.

My constant thanks to all my doctors, whose loving care has given me these years to be healthy in my Cancer World. They have encouraged me to write *There's Nothing Like a Breast, A Breast Cancer Survivor's Story of the Emotional and Sexual Effects of Reconstructive Surgery* and *Journey to Justice: A Woman's True Story of Breast Cancer and Medical Malpractice.*

Their patience, confidence, and support have been part of my lifeline for my good health. Dr. Braun Graham is my hero. Dr. Mark Moskowitz, my oncologist and friend since 1984, often mentioned that of all his patients, I was the one who would benefit most from reconstruction surgery. Dr. Paul Carbone, my precious oncologist and friend, could be counted on for understanding and encouragement. Dr. Richard Steeves, my fine radiation oncologist at UWCCC, relentlessly told me to go further with my writing and continually reassured me of the importance of what I had to say. Many thanks for the tools you gave me to succeed.

Dr. V. Craig Jordan, Diana Princess of Wales Professor of Cancer Research, and the Director, Lynn Sage Breast Cancer Research Program, the Tamoxifen developer, has been with me twice a day for almost seventeen years. Dr. Hiram "Chip" Cody III, from Sloan-Kettering Cancer Center, reminds me of my being a miracle.

Every Dec. 12 at 1 P.M. I call Chip to thank him for saving my life in 1983.

Thank you to all my doctors in Sarasota: Dr. Marie Velesco Ferrari, my internist; Dr. Carolyn Dixon, my gynecologist and confidante; and Dr. Thomas Schwartz, my ophthalmologist.

Thanks also to my wonderful Aunt Nish and Uncle George Finer, M.D. for always being with me.

Renee Schwartz protects me from legal liabilities in the literary field. Thanks for being with me all these years.

My mentor, Dr. John Royle, helped me create a strategic plan. My survival is bonded with John's faith in my abilities to succeed. His wife, Donna, has been my guardian angel.

My heart is never far from Linda Neu and the gracious home she opens to me when I visit in Madison.

Judy Mostovoy is another "miracle" in the sisterhood of cancer survivors. Her husband, Sheldon, is a "mensch" in the true meaning of the word.

Thank you to all my friends whose friendships have continued during so many years. They are: Howard Goldberg, Helen Baldwin, Carol Jefferson, Howard Goldman, Webster Chapman, Penny Aronson, Louise Fimlaid, Stella and Kelly George, Dottie and William Sloatman, Jean Cooper, Kim Fritzgerald, Mark Ray, Gale Fulton Ross, Gladys and Milton Yanow, Barbara and Hans Hospel, Diane Tyler, Sandy Larson Tumbutson, Brian Burant and Bette McCaulley, Rosemary Watson, Aviva Myers Woll, Tom W. Koopman Jr., Dr. Jay L. Friedland and Gail Chechik Wenocur.

Thanks to Barnes and Noble of Sarasota for their support with my book, *Journey to Justice*.

Many thanks to Debbie Dennis, Steve Lacy, Alice Fetcho, Noelle Bazell, Dominique Kersey, Sue Holleran, and Janice Monsen, Frank Troncale, Melanie Carling, Nancy R. Lane, Rebecca Ann Gardner, Merril Kargi, "peggy harris," Joanne E. "Jo" Mason, Deborah Lucas, Michael R. Martin, Carol Harlan, Nancy Finley, Hester Jeswald.

Also, thanks to Shirley Roskin, Ira Wiesner, Michael Hawkins, Lorry Eible of Foxy Lady Boutique,

Felice Goodman Levin, Nina Pinto, Cheryl Saladino, Mark Cunningham, Christine and Frank Heider, the late Emma Laughlin, Barbara and Karl Schten, Kay and Robert Gale, M.D., Sue and Harry Enstrom, Doug Seel, and, finally, Christopher Carroll, my public relations partner.

Many thanks to those numerous unmentioned people who have helped me.

It takes an army of support to fight for your life.

FOREWORD

Diane Chechik was one of the one in eight American women forced to face the diagnosis of breast cancer. Although the cause of breast cancer is not known, the often necessary surgical treatment—modified radical mastectomy—leaves behind not only physical scars but deep emotional wounds for women mourning the loss of their breast. This story is about Diane's emotional recovery from breast cancer and her discovery that for her, total "wellness" required reconstruction of her surgically removed breast. But this is not merely one woman's story; it is a tale of hope and health and transformation to which every woman can respond. Treatment for breast cancer may take several avenues: removal of the breast lump, followed by radiation therapy; total removal of the breast and lymph nodes under the arm (modified radical mastectomy); chemotherapy; hormonal therapy; or a combination of these. Then the patients are left with the long and lonely job of coming to terms with their mastectomy deformity. The surgical cure for breast cancer is sometimes small compensation for the loss of their body image.

Thousands of women agonize in front of a mirror each day, grieving at the ruination of their female form. They dress in the closet, embarrassed to be seen by their husband. Sadly, many women, out of touch with their feelings, pretend that the amputation of their breast is a trivial matter.

As a Plastic and Reconstructive Surgeon, I perform breast reconstruction for dozens of breast-cancer patients each year. Each woman has a unique set of circumstances, which dictates the course of her treatment. Despite the individuality of mastectomy patients, I see remarkably similar motivations in their decision for breast reconstruction: the yearning for restoration of the female form, the emotional need to "feel" like a woman, and the desire to suppress the fear of recurring breast cancer.

In recent years, plastic surgeons have successfully performed breast reconstruction immediately following the mastectomy, in order to spare patients the anguish of living without their breast. Approximately fifty percent of the breast reconstructive cases now performed are immediate reconstruction.

Although surgical reconstruction does nothing to alter long-term survival statistics, breast-cancer patients consider the emotional and psychological benefits valuable beyond measure. As a physician, I have been impressed by the profound impact that breast reconstruction has had on mastectomy patients regarding such everyday activities as wardrobe choice, especially swimwear, lingerie, and sportswear selection.

I met Diane Chechik eight years after her treatment for breast cancer. She had survived an advanced form of the disease requiring surgery, radiation therapy, chemotherapy, and hormonal therapy. She had recently published a book, *Journey to Justice,* detailing her horrible experience with delay in diagnosis and subsequent malpractice litigation. To those who knew Diane, she was vibrant, active, and well adjusted. To herself, she was miserably unhappy, living a lie, and stoically masking the heartache of her altered body image.

This book is about Diane's struggle to rid herself of the physical and emotional scars caused by breast cancer. She was struck by the epiphany that reconstruction of her amputated breast was essential to her sexuality and happiness. She realized that only by having a whole body could she leave cancer in the past and enjoy life again. Her honesty about suffering the loss of her femininity will be shared by most readers who have been treated for breast cancer. Her courageous willingness to delve into the connections among such intimate subjects as self-esteem, sexuality, womanliness, and well-being should provide physicians with great insight and enable them to deal more effectively and sensitively with the private concerns of breast cancer patients.

Diane's decision for reconstruction came at a time when the safety of silicone breast implants—used in breast reconstruction and breast enlargement procedures—was in question. Fortunately she was a candidate for breast reconstruction that utilized her own body tissues and was able to have her breast mound reconstructed entirely from excess skin and fat from the lower abdomen, without the need for an artificial implant device.

The incidence of breast cancer is rising. Our most effective treatments rely on early detection to optimize our chances of cure. Public education programs promoting aids to early detection have done much to increase women's awareness of the need for breast self-examination, routine physical examination, and mammograms. A better understanding of the procedures available to women for breast reconstruction may also contribute to their willingness to seek out evaluation of a breast lump they have noticed but chosen to ignore.

Diane's story echoes the emotions and needs of so many women treated for breast cancer. Not only is she an activist, she is a survivor. Her survival has enabled her to take a closer look at herself, restore her body, and face life with the confidence that her cancer is finally behind her.

Her search for wellness will empower many others to do the same.

Braun H. Graham, M.D., F.A.C.S.

Sarasota, Florida

DEDICATION

I dedicate *There's Nothing Like A Breast* to my late father, Maurice Craig (1909-1957), and my late mother, Dorothea (Dorothy)Craig (1909-1990). Many of my dad's words have been with me my entire life: "Don't ever let being a woman stop you from doing something."

My beautiful mother loved me with her heart and soul. Her heart was large for her family and friends, in spite of her physical heart problems.

Every day, I give them a kiss and tell them, "I love you and cherish being your devoted daughter."

This dedication is also to my remarkable sons, Marc David and Joel Craig, who have a unique way of constantly showing their concern for my health and happiness. I feel a responsibility to live up to their overwhelming expectations of me.

Sara, my beautiful and fine daughter-in-law, is truly a woman of grace. Sara has given me another way of being a mother through her loving care. Her self-esteem and success with her family, Joel, Lucy Anna, and Sonya Rose, gives me many happy moments of adoring her.

Lucy and Sonya, two beautiful granddaughters, are girls of outstanding abilities and elegance. They will define womanhood of the twenty-first century. Their eyes sparkle when they smile and say, "I love you, Grandma Diane."

My daughter-in-law Victoria, whose beauty radiates from her heart and soul through her physical being, has enriched Marc's heart and Samuel Joseph's and mine. Sam is a handsome, creative grandson. His laughter brings smiles to Grandma Diane.

AUTHOR'S NOTE

I've written *Journey to Justice: A Woman's True Story of Breast Cancer and Medical Malpractice* and *There's Nothing Like a Breast* to help guide you through your new world. Both books recount my experience that I found necessary for my survival. You'll learn how to fight, to persevere through your treatments, to interact with those in the Well World, and to explore and nurture your new selves— physical, emotional, and sexual.

Advances in technology for breast cancer treatment and diagnostic research will continue throughout the twenty-first century, increasing the membership in the breast-cancer sisterhood of survivors. Still, until a cure is found, one constant remains in spite of progress—the simple but sobering phrase, "You have breast cancer."

No one but a cancer survivor can comprehend the emotional trauma and life changes these words cause. Upon hearing them, a person leaves the Well World and is forever placed in the frightening, claustrophobic, and inescapable Cancer World.

The development of Tamoxifen® (Nolvadex) has been essential to my survival. (Tamoxifen is the most commonly administered antiestrogenic drug given to women with breast cancer. I believe that if I were to stop taking it, my cancer would recur.) I have taken it for sixteen years, having begun with one of the first test-trial groups in the country. Tamoxifen will be my partner for the rest of my life. While some authorities debate how long survivors must take Tamoxifen, my physicians know that if I go off it, most likely I would not survive a third occurrence. For me, the drug's most noticeable side effect is LIFE. (This is my experience, not an endorsement. Consult your medical oncologist.)

Three days a week, I walk Siesta Key beach. Golden rays shine through the new branches of my purple tree. It's a retreat into my imagination, a place of peace, privacy, and comfort where I sit and meditate and talk to God. I chose purple because it symbolizes passion and creativity, two cornerstones of my life. Its trunk is large and sturdy, a testimony to my survival. Its roots are secure. Its limbs are luminescent and lush with the many indigo leaves that have sprouted during my life.

The leaves blow in many directions, making music that sings to me. My purple tree branches move freely in the breezes of my life. They will not break in a storm. Their protection is my strength.

I created my tree when I was twelve years old. Since that time, it's been a refuge. When I moved to Siesta Key, Florida, from Madison, Wisconsin, my tree came with me. It reflects what is happening in my present life. The tree becomes fuller and more luxuriant, with strong limbs and glossy leaves, when my life seems healthy and happy and growing. When my world is troubled and chaotic, winter descends upon my place of peace.

Sitting under my tree now, I bask under blue sky and golden sunshine. As an exciting idea takes root in my mind, small buds begin to unfurl on a delicate, slender branch. It's a vision of my new self—yet another change is on the horizon.

The direction of my life has changed many times; often I want to resist this new possibility. Can't I stop and rest? As I gaze up at this majestic tree, courage washes over me.

While you fight cancer, find a tranquil and sheltering place where you can gather your thoughts, energies, and strength. It can be a real location or an imaginary one like mine, and it must serve as your symbol for hope, beauty, and life. From there you will have a view of your Cancer World welcoming you as a new member of the breast-cancer sisterhood.

When I visit my purple tree I find my visions of wellness, and meditate with God. With a sense of deep thankfulness for each day, I recognize the changes in my purple tree and myself. Some of its branches have separated and fallen. These branches represent my personal relationships whose foundations weakened. In their place, seedlings representing new relationships appear.

Join me under my purple tree. Together we will create more new branches as we take our refuge.

If my books contribute to the nurturing of breast-cancer survivors, then I have given back, with gratitude, the gift of my life to God, my family, friends, and friends I've yet to meet.

Diane Craig Chechik
Sarasota, Florida

"As you go the way of life, you will see a great chasm. Jump. It is not as wide as you think."

—Joseph Campbell
Reflections of Life

PROLOGUE

December 1993

Just nine years ago, I was a new divorcee, young, blonde, and sexy.

I had blue-green bedroom eyes, a small waist, and flowing hips perfectly proportioned to my petite frame. My breasts were round, tight, and beautiful.

For two years, I had enjoyed my life as a woman freed from a difficult marriage. Many fascinating men were eager to make me their own, but this wasn't the time for me to settle down. Life was too much fun.

But then, on March 29, 1982, I found a lump on my right breast. This frightened me. I thought I had breast cancer. My dad had died of cancer in 1957, and I was terrified it would claim me, too, before my fiftieth birthday, only five years away.

I went to see my doctor that afternoon. Bob Jackson had been my physician for seventeen years. After doing a needle aspiration of the lump, he reassured me that I was all right. After his examination, a mammogram was taken. He called to inform me that everything looked fine. There was no need for me to have a biopsy.

Three months later, I had another mammogram. Again Bob assured me that this was not breast cancer. He advised me to learn to live with the lump in my breast.

Exactly a year later, I went to another doctor for a physical exam, a requisite for employment with Aetna Casualty and Life Insurance Company. He asked me about the lump in my breast. I explained what Dr. Jackson had said and done.

"I defer to him," the physician told me.

Eight months later, I found a second lump, this one under my arm. This time, I felt certain that this was breast cancer. I told my sons, Joel and Marc, but they said, "Oh, Mom, there you go again. You don't have cancer." I tried to calm down.

A few days later, my mother became gravely ill. While dealing with the possibility of her death, I put off going to Bob Jackson about my second lump. What difference could a few more days make?

Thank goodness the infection around my mother's heart responded to medication, freeing me to see Bob. I told him that I wanted a biopsy with Dr. John Pellet at the University of Wisconsin Hospital and Clinic.

"You don't have cancer," Bob insisted, "and you don't need a biopsy. We'll watch the lump for ten days after your menstrual cycle ends, then we'll see. It'll probably go away the same way it came."

I was furious with Bob. I decided to go to New York City and visit my friend Felice. Shopping and partying might be just what I needed. Life's pressures were getting me down—the fear of having breast cancer preyed constantly on my mind.

In New York City, Felice convinced me to see a breast specialist, Dr. Hiram Cody III.

My appointment was for Monday, December 12, 1983. Dr. Cody performed a needle biopsy.

I had Stage Two-breast cancer.

"Your life is in danger," he told me. "You can have a mastectomy in New York or go home and have it done at the university hospital. Time is of the essence."

My greatest fear had become my reality.

At four o'clock I called Bob's office from Felice's apartment, so he could arrange for my admission to the hospital. Being with my boys, my family, and my friends was important to me.

Bob's nurse told me that he was with a patient. I told her this was an emergency. He came to the phone and asked, "Well, Diane, what's so important?"

After I told him the news, he insisted I did not have cancer. "What the hell are you doing in New York, seeing another doctor?" he demanded angrily.

Two days later, as I sat in Bob Jackson's office, he

called Dr. Cody in New York to confirm all my test results, then thanked him for taking such good care of me.

When Bob hung up the phone, he started to cry. "Oh, my God," he wept, "what have I done to you? But I just couldn't cut into your beautiful breast." He closed the office door, and we both cried.

"We'll get through this together, Diane," he promised. "I'm awfully glad you're going to have your surgery before I go on vacation to Hawaii."

PART ONE

CHAPTER 1

Five years had passed since my modified mastectomy. I sued Bob Jackson for medical malpractice and won. He never appealed the decision. I gained fifty-five pounds during the chemotherapy protocol and didn't even recognize my own body.

Five months after my last chemo session, I found another breast lump. It was malignant. After it was excised, I underwent radiation therapy.

I wrote about my experiences in a book entitled *Journey to Justice: A Woman's True Story of Breast Cancer and Medical Malpractice* and offered it free of charge to any public library in the United States. It was also issued in Braille and made available through the Helen Keller Braille Library in Hempstead, New York.

I decided to move to Florida. I had visited Sarasota with my family and fallen in love with the place. I knew I wanted to spend whatever time I had left living next to the Gulf of Mexico. My brush with death had taught me that dreams should never be postponed.

I urged my mother to move south with me, but she

refused. She was living in a nursing home and feared the move would be too much for her. I left without her but vowed that I would return often to see her.

Whenever I was in Wisconsin, I would schedule examinations with my doctors. One, Paul Carbone, had been my medical oncologist and was the director, professor, and chairman of the Department of Human Oncology at the University of Wisconsin Comprehensive Cancer Center. He wrote the foreword to my book and testified in my behalf at the malpractice proceedings.

Another was my radiation research oncologist, Eric Meyer. When I began my series of thirty radiation treatments, he introduced himself in a soft voice, with his hands outstretched to grasp mine. He mentioned that he would be overseeing my treatments and monitoring my progress. He assured me that he would have the medical staff and radiation physicians administer the same fine care that I was being given by Dr. Carbone. Whenever Eric came in to see me, his sparkling eyes and warm, friendly manner provided a welcome contrast to a room of cold, large, mechanical devices whose harsh buzzing sounded in my dreams and woke me in a cold sweat. Eric's smile showed off his dimples and almost perfect teeth. His black hair was straight and just beginning to show some gray, which only emphasized his youthful good looks. He would hug me at the end of every session and say, "You'll be fine,

Diane." This wasn't unusual for Eric; he hugged most of his women patients.

Eric called me periodically after my relocation, to ask how I was feeling. He often talked about his research, patients, and work. I was surprised and pleased by the attention this handsome, successful man bestowed on me.

One time, in 1989, he called sounding very upset. He said that he knew he could trust me and confided some of his personal problems. He wanted to talk about how I handled my divorce. This was his first mention of anything personal. For a moment I thought he was telling me too much about his private life; then I felt flattered that he would share his feelings so openly.

He thanked me for listening and asked when I planned to come back for a visit; he missed seeing me. His gentle concern and frequent calls helped me to feel more connected to my faraway health-care providers.

Following one telephone conversation I realized that not making local contacts in case I needed emergency treatment was irresponsible. Deciding to familiarize myself with the Sarasota medical community, I signed up for a Breast Cancer Update seminar in January, 1989, sponsored by the Sarasota Memorial Hospital.

There, the panel of eight doctors discussed all aspects of breast cancer and reconstructive surgery. As I listened to Dr. Braun Graham, a plastic surgeon, something stirred inside me, and I underlined his name on the program, then encircled it with five stars. I noticed that his hometown was Indianapolis, Indiana. A Midwesterner like me, I thought. I was impressed by his soft manner, sensitive choice of words, empathetic approach to the subject of breast cancer, and his obvious respect for women. Maybe someday I'll have reconstruction, I thought with longing. Then I chuckled at my foolishness. I was lucky to be alive! Why would I want to risk surgery for the sake of vanity? My loneliness was one reason, if I was willing to admit it. I bristled at the truth: The men I dated now were less wonderful than the fellows I had known before my mastectomy. Since then, whenever men expressed even a mild interest in me, I prepared myself for rejection, for their being turned off by my cancer.

I told myself that their response was a rejection of my condition, not of me personally. But sometimes I just wanted to say, You go to hell! Having cancer isn't enough? Now I have to be spurned for it?

No matter what the risk, I was always truthful— the men I went out with had to know the state of my health and my distorted body well before we reached the bedroom or even thought about making love. Even after they knew and promised they didn't care, I always suffered from anxiety. I would take a deep breath and pray my partner could deal with my appearance and the feel of my scars under his fingertips.

I had little time to think about that seminar or myself as a candidate for breast reconstruction. My mother's health was rapidly deteriorating. I went up to see her in March, then again in April and early May. I knew this was going to be our last visit. Mother could not fight any longer.

During those heartrending days, Eric frequently came upstairs from the research lab to visit me in Mom's hospital room. He reminded me that he was my friend, and if I needed his help, he would be ready. He expressed concern about how the stress and exhaustion were affecting my health. He held me while I cried. His kindness was without bounds.

Mom's doctors sent her back to the nursing home to die. I rode in the ambulance with her and held her hand. I asked her through my tears, "Please don't die on Mother's Day," which was the next day.

Mom laughed weakly and said, "I'll see what I can arrange."

She worried about our being separated. She knew she would have to take her final journey without me. She and I loved each other so much and shared the special bond of having suffered a severe illness. During my battle with cancer, she had committed herself to keeping me alive through her spirit, love, and caring. In the last few months, I had done the same for her. Now she thanked me for being a good daughter who had fought for her life. I told her she had been a wonderful mother.

I began to feel very much alone. As if she had read my thoughts, she told me not to repeat her mistake of never remarrying after my father's death. I promised her that when the right man came around, I would marry him.

Mom honored my request. In her last moments of life she inquired about the time. It was 12:05 A.M., Monday, May 14, the day after Mother's Day. We kissed, and I thanked her for staying alive another twenty-four hours. She smiled and kissed me again. We said, "I love you," then she fell asleep as I held her in my arms. Soon she was gone.

I needed to be with my sons after Mom's death. I thought a lot about motherhood and the fact that someday Joel and Marc would lose me. As I grieved for my mother, I found myself mourning other losses in my life. Every day I looked at my body, my breast, and my scar, and felt bereft.

I spent a few days with Marc in St. Louis, Missouri. Then I went to Minneapolis to see Joel and my daughter-in-law, Sara. They helped me to heal, and I returned to Florida feeling a little better.

As the months went by, I struggled to lead a normal existence. I was an orphan. My caregiving days were over. I felt frighteningly alone. I had to take stock of my new role in life.

For five years my days had been a succession of doctor's appointments, blood tests, radiation, chemotherapy, and medical protocol. I tried to accept what had happened to me and my body and remain optimistic about the future. I worked to put a determinedly happy face on things. But as the pain of my mother's death lessened from a sharp stab to a dull ache, the unhappiness I felt about my lost breast worsened. The fact remained glaringly obvious that I was wearing Bob Jackson's negligence between my throat and my waist. His malfeasance had changed every aspect of my life. My prosthesis was my constant burden of his guilt.

I realized with a jolt that Bob's influence on my life was more enduring than my ex-husband's had been. When I divorced, I was essentially finished except for some tangled legalities and minor annoyances. Bob, however, would be with me forever—every morning he was in the shower with me as I lathered my misshapen body. Whenever I wore a bathing suit, his ghostly presence handed me the prosthesis to stuff into my bodice. Whenever I made love, the specter of Bob Jackson stood by the bed while my partner tentatively touched my mastectomy scar. His failure loomed over my life. And I was infuriated by it. I wanted him out!

Even though I had won a settlement from him in court, it wasn't enough. I did not feel as if justice had been served.

I was experiencing a radical shift in attitude. For the first time in many years I began to believe from my very soul that I was going to beat cancer. The seemingly endless treatments were behind me. My hair had grown back, and I was able to lose some weight. But in spite of my progress in other areas, a new breast would not spontaneously regenerate.

I studied and organized my finances; I was spending more money than I was earning. Tellingly, up until this time I believed that I would not be alive for very long so, I thought, why not spend my money and enjoy what time I had?

Eric called several times during the summer to ask about my health. His father had died some years before, so he understood what I was going through. He encouraged me to rest and do special things for myself.

The idea of giving myself a treat led to thoughts about Dr. Graham. Eric spoke often of the importance of conserving the breast, and whenever the subject had come up, I was shaken by sudden and unexpected anger. Had my cancer been diagnosed properly, I might have had the option of a lumpectomy and radiation, rather than the drastic measures I had been forced to endure.

Now I casually mentioned reconstructive surgery. Eric seized on the idea of our discussing it—in Madison. I told him no and explained my plan to choose a local physician. Now that Mom was gone, I explained, I probably wouldn't be flying up to Wisconsin very often. He seemed extremely disappointed to hear that.

After we hung up, I felt depressed and didn't know why. I went for soothing walk on the beach. I sat on the sugary sand and found comfort under my purple tree as I allowed myself to feel my aloneness. I was dating but didn't feel anything special for the men. I wondered what I was going to do with my life. I gazed up through the golden branches and dreamed of meeting a special someone—a professional man, handsome, well educated, gentle, and sensitive. Exactly like Eric.

In June, an acquaintance invited me to her house for dinner. She wanted me to autograph my book for her daughter, who had breast cancer. She asked if she might invite a man to meet me. I thought that would be fine; I've always believed that I would meet my next husband through friends.

David Finkel was a funny, nice-looking New Yorker with big blue eyes, dimples, and a receding hairline. I enjoyed meeting him, and apparently he felt the same way about me. He was divorced. I told him I was a cancer survivor. We talked on the phone many times during the week without his asking me out for a date. I couldn't understand why.

Eric's next phone call surprised me. He asked if I

would like some company for a weekend in October. I knew I could use the diversion, and I thought I would like to see him. I was lonely. I told him yes; we had developed a sincere friendship. Over the weeks our telephone conversations had become more frequent. I never noticed any flirtatiousness, but I wasn't looking for it. Eric continued to affirm his wanting a change.

He called me often during the next three weeks. He wanted to assure me that he was thinking of me. His voice was different than before—softer and almost intimate.

CHAPTER 2

Eric arrived on October 19. We hugged at the airport. I was so glad to see him. During our drive to my condo, he caught me up on Madison gossip and how things were going at the hospital. He was enthusiastic about my move to Sarasota, especially when he realized that I lived only a block from the Gulf of Mexico.

Eric set his luggage down inside my front door, turned to me, and kissed me for what seemed like forever. Despite all the months of phone calls and letters to each other, I was caught entirely off guard. Either I hadn't been able to admit what was growing between us or I felt so strongly about not becoming involved with a married man that I ignored all the signs.

Now I swayed breathless in his arms, closed my eyes, and accepted the soft sweetness of his lips. It had been so long since a man had kissed me like that. I had been alone, so alone.

As he broke off the kiss and moved back a step to smile down at me, I told myself I could handle the situation. I just needed to keep a cool head. How complicated could it be, I thought, with our living so far apart? I knew he wasn't happy; it wasn't as if I would be coming between him and his wife.

With all my excuses and rationalizations, the truth was that Dr. Eric Meyer was too good for me to say no to. Besides his obvious and many attributes, he was a man to whom a breastless woman was as normal as a dollar bill to a banker. He wouldn't flinch or find me repulsive when I took off my clothes.

I did not want to jump to conclusions, however. Maybe he was planning to take things slowly. I showed him to my guest room. He laughed and informed me that he was going to be sleeping with me in my bedroom. Then he kissed me again. Feeling suddenly shy, I fled to the kitchen and gabbled nervously. I handed him a glass of fresh-squeezed orange juice, told him that an affair might not be such a good idea, offered him an apple crisp I had baked, then outlined our schedule for the rest of the day. He drank the juice, declined the crisp, and told me that my nervousness was adorable.

After Eric changed into light, casual clothes, we went to St. Armands Circle with its elegant shops, then ate lunch at the posh Cafe L'Europe. We toured Mote Marine Laboratory, then the beach. Once, Eric stopped and kissed me, and I heard the winds and the waves play a song for us. We talked and laughed and held hands. People we passed smiled at our obvious happiness. At around four in the afternoon, Eric said he'd like to rest for a while, so I brought him home. While he took a shower, I sat at my kitchen counter and thought about all the reasons why he and I shouldn't be lovers. Foremost among them was the fact that my former husband had cheated on me for twenty-two years. I had never been involved with a married man. I didn't wanted to hurt another woman the way I had been hurt. And I didn't want to give my love in trust to an unfaithful man.

The old sorrow and anger tore at my heart. I had made a pact in 1975 in a last-ditch attempt to save our marriage by giving up my interior-design business, and he'd be faithful.

"Diane, are you going to join me?"

Eric's voice startled me from my memories. I was grateful for the interruption. I walked into the bedroom and found him in my bed.

"Are you going to join me?" he repeated, and patted the bed.

"I-I'm not sure," I answered, and sat on the edge of the mattress and looked at him, my buddy.

Eric reached under my pillow and pulled out a bottle of perfume, which he had hidden there for me. I opened it, sniffed it, and made all the appropriate polite noises. He kissed me again.

"Come on, Diane, get in beside me. Everything is going to be all right. You and I will be friends for our lifetime."

"No, we won't," I told him. "You just want our weekend together."

"You're wrong, honey." He sat up and tilted my chin so he could look into my eyes. "This is new to me—you're new to me—but someday you and I will be together. Thinking of being here with you all of the time instead of settling for the phone calls and letters—that's what's kept me going." He kissed me again, gently, little kisses on my lips, my forehead, my eyes, while he whispered, "Come here, Diane, and let me love you."

I finally fell tearfully into Eric's embrace because I was tired of fighting against something I wanted so much. He accepted me, as I was—both my mind and my body. Nobody else in my life offered me such unconditional approval. I had taken delight in lovemaking until my breast was lopped off. Now, being with Eric was like turning back the clock to my carefree days of good health and a whole body. He didn't care that I had one breast.

But more than anything else, after so many years of battling for my life—with chemo and drains and scars and radiation burns and pills and baldness and my prosthesis—I wanted to be loved. I deserved to be loved! This was my time, at last, to lie back, relax in a man's arms, and feel pleasure.

The weekend was filled with talking and laughing, long walks on the moonlit beach, romantic dinners, bubble baths and champagne, and passionate love. We talked about his research and my writing. We talked about the future. He told me he had waited years, ever since he first met me, for this moment. That came as a revelation.

We seemed so right for each other that I quashed my doubts and guilt. Having a wonderful, charming lover went along with my new confidence that I had a future.

When we said good-bye at the airport on Sunday, Eric asked me to join him in December in California, where he would be attending a medical convention.

I could have agreed immediately and made it easy for him, but I couldn't do that to myself. I thanked him for the wonderful, loving weekend, then took a deep breath and told him I would not be joining him in California.

"You must change your status," I urged him, "just like I did. Be honest with yourself. If you can do that, then I'll see you again."

He pulled me into his arms and kissed the top of my head. "I'm going to try to change your mind," he said into my hair. "When I'm with you, I'm in ecstasy."

I believed him. I felt the same way with him. Besides, why else would a man who could have any woman he wants fly a thousand miles to see me—middle-aged, a bit worse for wear, and missing a breast?

CHAPTER 3

Eric called me at least once a week, and his cards were adoring. He wanted to pursue our relationship, but I remained steadfast. I would not join him in California.

There was no joy is my decision. I felt no satisfaction from my self-righteousness. I was lonely and sad and bitter about what I was depriving myself of, all in ethical and moral consideration of not seeing a married man.

The one thing I did agree to do with Eric was collaborate on a magazine article about prostate and breast cancers. I went to the Sarasota Memorial Hospital Medical Library to read current articles, and Eric helped by sending me research, giving me guidance, and answering my questions.

A second article, all mine, evolved from the first. It focused on the benefits I enjoyed by remaining sexually active after my mastectomy. I believed—or at least I thought I did—that lovemaking provided a connection to the world of wellness and served as a between-the-sheets affirmation of the life force still burning brightly within me.

Whenever a man took me to bed in the early days after my surgery, I congratulated myself for managing to feel sexy and attracting a lover in spite of my chest of scars. When I was in the throes of orgasm, I forgot about my cancer. *See?* I'd tell myself. *Breast cancer isn't so bad after all!*

A well-known national men's magazine expressed interest in the article and sent me on a second round of research. My search for up-to-date materials brought me back in contact with Braun Graham, the plastic surgeon who had impressed me so favorably at the hospital-sponsored seminar a year before.

I called his office and was invited in to watch informational videotape about reconstructive surgery. I sat with his head nurse, Susan Tyler, in a beautifully appointed, dimly lit viewing room. One wall displayed certificates and diplomas for Dr. Graham and his partner, Dr. James Schmidt, including their certificates from the American Society for Aesthetic Plastic Surgery and the American Society of Plastic Surgeons.

Dr. Schmidt and Dr. Graham met at the University of Florida, in Gainesville, during their residency in plastic surgery in 1983. Jim is a graduate of the University of Wisconsin Medical School. Braun graduated from Indiana University Medical Center.

Susan handed me several booklets and brochures,

then started the videotape. Dr. Graham appeared on the television screen and explained clearly and simply the surgical options available to women and what each entailed. I scribbled notes across my legal pad. My writing trailed off, and I watched in stunned silence as images of women whose breasts had been reconstructed showed on the screen. I shifted in my seat, and I leaned forward, my eyes riveted to picture after picture of mutilation, then beauty; mutilation, then beauty; mutilation, then . . .

Thunderstruck by the magnificence of what Dr. Graham had been able to accomplish for these women, I sank weakly back into the chair. My prosthesis pinned me down like a lead weight.

"Diane, are you all right?" Susan asked.

I could hardly find my voice. "Fine," I told her. "Just . . . tired, I guess."

"Can I get you some water?"

"No. I-I'm fine." I took a deep breath. "Would you mind if I stayed and watched the tape a couple more times?"

"Of course not," she said kindly. "Come and get me when you're done." Then she left me alone to wrestle with my past and my future.

I was more than tired, and I wasn't fine; but I didn't understand the feelings that were churning inside me. I tried to watch the videotape again, but seeing those women with their beautiful breasts was too painful for me.

I had written an article for *Ladies' Home Journal* that defiantly stated that a mastectomy was not a mutilation; it was simply the removal of a diseased body part. Now, sitting in that chair, for the first time I felt mutilated.

I snatched up my belongings, thanked the nurses at their desk, and fled from the office.

A surprise phone call awaited me on my answering machine when I got home. David Finkel had called to invite me for a walk on the beach. Since our mutual friends had introduced us weeks before, we had become telephone pals; but we never dated and rarely saw each other.

I called him back, and we set up a time to get together.

David appeared promptly at my front door. We went across the street to Siesta Key Beach. My spirits lifted; the beach always has that effect on me. As we walked, he held my hand.

"Diane, I think it's time we changed our relationship into something more real," he said without preamble.

I nearly stumbled in the sand. He meant sex. I told him no, that I wanted him as a friend, not a lover. He accepted my answer with good grace, and we had a nice evening.

Later, when I was alone, I thought about David's proposition. I didn't need more complications in my life. I already had a lover . . . sort of.

But, I told myself, you don't have anyone else in your life in Sarasota. You and David have a warm friendship for a foundation. And whom are you kidding about Eric? Your affair with him is limited to the telephone lines.

During the next week, David called every night, stopped in for coffee, and brought over the makings of dinner. He was affectionate with a hello kiss. We cooked together while listening to Cleo Lane tapes. We both loved jazz. At dinner, he reached across the table and touched my hands. He was attentive to the conversation, and we laughed loudly and often. His warmth captivated me.

Our friendship was becoming a romance. After a couple more weeks of courtship, David put his arms around me, held me tenderly, and kissed me deeply. We both responded with a passion that hadn't existed before. He kept saying he cared for me.

Finally, we made love the next Saturday afternoon. I never slid into bed with great expectations. Disrobing in front of David for the first time made me feel anxious.

I tried to keep a light tone to my voice, but the heaviness was in my heart.

My mind flicked to the videotape I had watched earlier that day, and an unexpected fury shook me. *Don't be stupid,* I told myself. You should be happy you're alive.

Later, David and I showered, got dressed, and went to the movies. I reached over in the dark and took his hand.

CHAPTER 4

I did not miss the irony that while I was polishing a magazine article about how great lovemaking was after breast cancer, I was simultaneously questioning why the men in my life were so wrong for me. Having a piece published in a national men's magazine would be a wonderful career achievement; the topic of healthy sex for mastectomy victims could result, I thought, in a talk-show appearance. Oprah Winfrey's staff had contacted me about an appearance after *Journey to Justice* was issued in Braille, and the publication of the magazine article could serve as the impetus to get me on her show.

In spite of that, as I labored on my final round of revisions as outlined by the magazine's senior editor, I felt no enthusiasm for the project. Outrage over the influence of cancer and Bob Jackson's misdiagnosis surfaced as I tried to write and would destroy my concentration. In desperation, as my deadline neared, I hired a free-lance book editor to help me.

Laurie Rosin had worked in publishing in New York

for thirteen years before moving to Sarasota. She had fifty million copies in print with Bantam and thirty national bestsellers under her belt. I felt hopeful that she would be able to pull out of me the words and phrases that seemed impossibly blocked.

As she and I worked together, we became friends. Eric came for a visit, and the three of us met and conferred. Laurie encouraged me to elaborate on some points and be more specific in certain areas. I tried my best but drew a blank. I couldn't remember many details.

"Sex was great," I told her by rote. "The men were gentle and understanding. It was a learning experience for everyone."

"You weren't sensitive about how you looked?"

"No! I was glad to be alive! A breast is a small price to pay for life."

Laurie narrowed her eyes and in a quiet voice asked me one simple question. "Tell me the truth, Diane. How was it *really?*"

At that moment, all my forbidden thoughts and feelings from the last eight years blasted into my consciousness. I burst into tears. "It was awful," I wailed. "It was horrible." That was the first time I had ever uttered those words. My sobs tore out of me with a force that frightened us both. Laurie jumped out of her chair and rushed to put her arms around me. She held me while I cried.

I finally admitted that the article was nothing but a lie. I had been trying to portray myself as some sort of carefree femme fatale in a satin boa and red high-heeled shoes, when in reality I had been constantly nauseated from chemotherapy and chafed by my underpants because my pubic hair had fallen out. My perspiration had smelled like medicine. What did I know about enjoying sex with masterful partners? I had been battling to survive, and the men had treated me like medical waste. I thought they were all I deserved. If I hadn't had cancer, I asked myself now, would I have chosen these men? The answer was no.

For the first time, I knew my chest was ugly. "Oh, God," I keened, "what has happened to me?"

I didn't want the magazine article to be published but felt it was too late for me to withdraw it from consideration. I prayed the magazine would reject it at the last minute, but that was unlikely; by this point in the process, ninety-nine percent of the stories were accepted.

My breakdown and admitting the truth of my feelings was a turning point in my life. My identity was all wrong. I didn't know this person I had become, shaped by a doctor's mistake. I was tired of working so hard to seem nonchalant when I disrobed. I was done with seeing the wrong men and living with a wrong body, with the real person hidden inside me. I wanted to have me back, away from my breast cancer. I wanted to feel accepted and wanted. And I wanted my breast back.

I had begun the journey for my other breast.

Much to my surprise, David continued to call. He talked about his business and family.

Then, just when I began to feel warmly toward him, he expressed concern that I might be caring more for him than he was for me. I found this incredible. I wanted to kick myself for going to bed with him. I reminded David that changing our relationship had been his idea, not mine.

In disgust, I told David good-bye and decided that the next time Eric called me, I would accept his invitation to meet him, no matter where. It made more sense to me to risk being hurt sometime in the future by a man who treated me like a goddess than to be treated inconsiderately by David. Besides, Eric was like a happy kid when we were together; I knew our love would grow. Most important, I didn't want to risk his losing interest in me or finding someone closer to home.

Because I had gone through a divorce, I knew I could help Eric during his difficult time ahead. He had certainly helped me when I was in treatment. If things didn't work out between us, we could go back to being just friends. Or maybe we'd find out that we were soulmates and be together forever.

He called two days later, and I agreed to meet him

in February 1991, at Disney World—the perfect place to live a fantasy.

Feeling honor bound to finish the magazine article, I went back to Dr. Graham's office and interviewed Susan Tyler for almost an hour. She asked me about my breast cancer, and I mentioned my book. I felt a little awkward about saying the word *malpractice*. Some physicians had refused to take me on as a patient when they found out I had sued a doctor.

I asked if I could see the videotape about reconstructive surgery once more. I had to be sure I got all the information—or perhaps I wanted to see it again because of my own needs and curiosity. Susan started the tape, then left me alone. I played it back in parts and yearned to feel my breast again. Bob's words haunted me, *I could not cut into your beautiful breast. . . .* I could not cut into your beautiful . . .

Finally, I had seen my fill. I found Susan, thanked her for her time, and as I walked out the door I offhandedly mentioned, "Maybe I'll come back as a patient."

I finished my final revisions on the cursed article and sent it by FedEx to the magazine's senior editor in New York. I felt exhausted and hypocritical. One thing I've always loved about *Journey to Justice* is its honesty. Women from across the country had written to thank me for saving their life and for letting them know they weren't alone. I believed I was betraying their trust with my newest effort. When this article hit the newsstands, those same women would wonder why they were suffering psychic pain while I, at the same point in my recovery, had been whooping it up with multiple orgasms.

I went into a funk. My self-esteem was shot. I had beaten cancer, but I was losing another battle, for myself. I was keeping myself from moving on to a new life.

I began to ask myself, Why do I have to live with this body if I'm going to live for a long time? I don't want to grow old with one breast. And I am going to grow old!

I thought of the tapes in Dr. Graham's office. I wanted to have reconstructive surgery. Could I afford it? Was it a waste of money on vanity? What would my friends say? What would Joel and Marc think?

Should I do it?

Why the hell not?

PART TWO
CHAPTER 5

Now that I was seriously considering breast reconstruction, I was eager to discuss it with someone I respected who would give me an objective opinion. I chose Dr. Paul Carbone. I credit his quick action and medical protocol with saving my life after my mastectomy, and I respect him as a person as well as a physician. (*Good Housekeeping* magazine has named him as one of the best doctors in America.)

Fortuitously, it was about the time for me to fly north for my six-month checkup at the University of Wisconsin Comprehensive Cancer Center. I made reservations to leave immediately so I could attend the funeral services for a friend who had died of prostate cancer. I contacted my sons so they could arrange to meet me in Madison.

The Wisconsin weather was bleak. I sat in the clinic waiting room and glanced at the many people whose complexions were as gray as the clouds on that winter day. Probably in the grip of chemo and radiation, those patients wanted nothing more than to survive. Feeling guilty for wanting so much more than that now, I decided that there are many levels of survival and that I was at a point of needing to move forward to keep my sanity.

In the weeks since finishing the magazine article about breast cancer and healthy sex, I had dealt with free-flowing anger. I'd stalked around my house, and nothing pleased me—except the very welcome and unexpected news that the article had miraculously been rejected at the last moment.

The magazine's senior editor returned a copy of my work to me, complimented the quality of the writing, explained that the publisher had decided to put more emphasis on political current events as opposed to personal experiences, and wished me good luck in placing the piece elsewhere.

I nearly fainted with relief. I knew I would never submit the article to another magazine; the work had served its purpose by dredging up the past, pushing me into Dr. Braun's office, and razing the foundation of lies on which I had built my postmastectomy life. But now that my house of cards had been torn down, nothing was left but the rage I had suppressed for eight years. Of course I knew that venting it was healthy, but it wasn't much fun living inside my skin.

I changed my hairstyle monthly—a different salon,

a new hairdresser. My need to alter my appearance was simply a manifestation of my frustration and self-dissatisfaction.

I couldn't get comfortable with my *bodyself,* as I called it. I felt ugly. I couldn't escape the reminder of my cancer and Bob Jackson's malfeasance. I was obsessed with wanting two breasts. Only then would I be well again, with Dr. Jackson banished from my life.

Thoughts of reconstruction surgery consumed me. Florida's spring comes early, and as I wore my bathing suits more often, my body image became more a problem. I resented being forced by my prosthesis to wear one-piece, old-fashioned swimsuits when my taste favored two-piece sets in reds and purples.

One day as I was getting ready to go swimming during one of Eric's visits, I picked up my prosthesis and, with a passion equal to our lovemaking, screamed and threw the hated rubber insert against the wall.

"No way!" I yelled. "I am not wearing this damned thing again!"

Eric, still in my bed, looked at me in surprise, then asked if he had done something to upset me.

I flopped down next to him, and tears of frustration burned my eyes. Embarrassed by my tantrum, I could only shake my head. I think I had been overwhelmed by the contrast between feeling so perfect while we had made love and so ugly while stuffing the prosthesis inside my swimsuit.

Eric pulled me close to comfort me. He was visiting frequently now that I had given him the go-ahead. He assured me that I was the sexiest woman he had ever met. I had, he said, a "beautiful chest wall." He caressed me and pulled down my swimsuit straps, but I didn't feel romantic. My misery with my looks precluded lovemaking. My body was out of balance with my soul. Eric was taken aback by my pain. Somehow, we fell asleep and after we awoke from our nap, went out for dinner. Neither one of us ever mentioned my outburst again. Nor did I tell him that I was seriously considering plastic surgery. Eric liked me too much just as I was.

Now, as a nurse led to me an examining room, I felt nervous, like a child who wanted her father's approval— no, blessings!—to do something she knew he wouldn't like. I was hurting. On my next visit to Madison, I wanted Paul Carbone to hear my cry for help. I thought he could stop my pain by listening and offering his consent.

I sat on the table and felt alone. I felt like a breast-cancer victim. I knew I was not going to feel that way any longer.

I'd mentioned reconstructive surgery to him in the past, and he had advised against it. I'm not sure of all the reasons, but like most people, Dr. Carbone considered it to be unnecessary surgery. He thought I was doing fine without a breast. I was extremely well adjusted. Right? Wrong! Not anymore.

Paul apologized for his delay, saying that he was having an unusually busy morning. While he was examining me, I started to explain everything that was on my mind.

He looked up from writing my prescription for Tamoxifen for six months and said, "You're doing well, and you look great. But if you are feeling a need to have reconstructive surgery, then I'll support you. I just want you to be healthy and happy." His understanding gave me a feeling of inner peace.

From the hospital, I drove to the Frank Lloyd Wright Unitarian Church for a memorial of a poet friend of mine who died of cancer. The lowering clouds were darker now, and snowflakes blew against my face as I walked into the church.

"Are you Diane Craig Chechik?"

I turned to look into the brown eyes of a tall, beautiful woman with auburn hair. "Yes." "The author of *Journey to Justice?*"

"Yes."

She threw her arms around my neck. "You saved my life," she said, then stepped back and smiled. "I'm Winona Ruehl. May I talk with you for a few minutes?"

"Of course." The snow was coming down harder,

and a wind was clutching at my coat. "Would you mind sitting in the car? It's over there."

"Fine."

We held on to each other and made our way carefully across the slick pavement. Why do people live here? I wondered, thinking of my green gulf and blue-gray herons. Once we were cocooned in my snow-covered rental car, I turned on the ignition and the heater.

"Diane, in the spring of 1984, I found a lump in my breast. My doctor told me that it was probably scar tissue from a breast implant that had been removed. Guess who? . . ."

"C. Robert Jackson," I said with certainty as a shiver crawled up my spine.

Winona nodded. "I went back to him six months later for another general exam. The lump was still there. He continued telling me I was all right."

"Dear God," I murmured.

"My husband saw you being interviewed on television, and he found your book for me. While reading it, I made an appointment to see a surgeon and asked for a biopsy. It was breast cancer. I underwent a modified radical mastectomy."

I had no words.

Winona had considered bringing a malpractice suit against Jackson, but because the cancer had miraculously not progressed beyond an early stage, she believed she could not win.

"If it hadn't been for you and your book," she said, reaching across the seat and squeezing my hand, "I probably would not be here now."

As we sat together, we realized that often we were part of the recent statistics for breast cancer. We knew some of our girlfriends will be part of the 175,000 new cases diagnosed each year. We were working toward not being counted among the 44,500 who die each year. One in every eight women will be diagnosed with this disease in her lifetime.

I told Winona that I felt my mission in writing *Journey* was to save women's lives and breasts. Every time I've helped someone, I felt that much stronger myself. I've received letters of gratitude from women all over the country who, trusting in their physician's diagnosis, were walking around with a time bomb in their breast. Also, I told her many patients whose doctors have trivialized the discovery of a breast lump often took a copy of *Journey to Justice* to their physician.

Both of us wondered why misdiagnosis occurs, especially when so many tests exist for determining whether an abnormality is benign or malignant. One is a simple procedure called a *needle biopsy* and can be done right in the doctor's office.

We shared our feelings that it is incumbent upon all women to be responsible for their own health care. Women must carefully examine their breasts every month to become completely familiar with their anatomy and detect any new lumps at the earliest possible time. Monthly self-examinations and annual mammograms after the age of thirty-five are essential because an early diagnosis gives a woman options in regard to her treatment. Early detection improves the possibility of surviving breast cancer and is most likely to lead to minimal surgery (that is, a lumpectomy followed by radiation therapy).

An alarmingly small percentage of women—only fifteen percent—diagnosed with breast cancer seek a second opinion. A second opinion is advisable even if the patient is satisfied with the first doctor's report and recommendation. Women diagnosed as having a malignancy should seek out a surgeon experienced in performing *lumpectomies,* which can preserve the breast, and modified radical mastectomies. And the patient should look for a surgeon who will be sensitive to her anxieties.

Winona and I sat for a long time. Finally, we hugged, and I wished her luck. We exchanged addresses and phone numbers and promised to keep in touch.

One month later, during another visit to Madison, Winona and I met for lunch in a Chinese restaurant. She asked me if I wanted to see what her breast looked like, with the implant. I said yes. We retreated to the ladies' room and locked ourselves inside. She showed me her breast, and I showed her what was left of mine. She urged me to consider reconstruction and offered to make an appointment for me with her plastic surgeon.

As we stood there, bare-breasted and giggling like embarrassed schoolgirls, intimate and trusting and yet relative strangers, I was struck by how the common bond of breast cancer had connected us in an everlasting friendship.

That evening, Joel flew to Madison from Minneapolis, and Marc came in from St. Louis.

Joel worked as a fund-raiser, and his wife, Sara, had just taken a position with a new company in sales. They were saving money so he could open his own business.

Marc had been hired for an exciting new position as senior writer with a fine advertising agency. He had many old friends from his years at the University of Missouri School of Journalism. And this new challenge would be good for him.

I wasn't planning to mention the plastic surgery to them, but I did want to lay the groundwork and convey the fact that I was undergoing changes. We met in my hotel room, then went to dinner at our favorite place, Smoky's, which I think has the best steaks in Madison.

Over dinner, I told them that I had talked with Dr. Carbone about my having reconstruction surgery.

"About what?" they asked, startled, and I realized that I had to be honest with them. I had never kept anything from them in the past—they even knew all about my affair with Eric—and they had been steadfastly by my side throughout the cancer ordeal. They deserved nothing less than my complete openness.

When I explained my need for plastic surgery, both Marc and Joel were glad I had talked with Paul. They suggested that I just might be going through a phase because I wanted to look good for Eric. They told me that my beauty had nothing to do with having one breast. After all, I had my life.

"Please listen," I cut in. "I did think that way for eight years. But now I feel differently."

They were worried about my having more surgery "just for a breast." "It's more than a breast," I explained. "I need to feel whole in order to survive in my new life. I'm unable to function positively. My feelings of dissatisfaction are too strong."

Marc and Joel urged me to wait before I did anything so drastic.

"I'm a different person," I told them, feeling desperate. A metamorphosis was taking place, I explained. Being born was a woman who at one time had suffered breast cancer—not a lifelong cancer victim.

"Are you listening?"

They nodded yes.

Then the next afternoon, they got on their airplanes and went home. We didn't speak about reconstructive surgery again.

Eric and I had dinner together after the boys left.

In the hotel room he administered a most unprofessional physical examination with his magic, gentle fingers.

I decided to tell Eric about the surgery. I shared my feeling of melancholy because of my boys' reaction. He shrugged and said he had no opinion. Because he deals with cancer every day, he views a cancer-ravaged body from a unique perspective. He told me to think about it carefully before undergoing major surgery.

Eric was cold to me and nervous in his home territory. Only when we were alone in my hotel room and making love did he act like himself. Of course his anxiety was perfectly understandable.

But the fact of our skulking around did not rest comfortably on top of my experiences of the last two days.

I told Eric that I wanted to stop our affair. He became very upset and pleaded with me to give him more time. He loved me so much, he said. Soon we would be together all the time. Eric assured me that he was the man of my life, and our futures were inextricably entwined.

By the time I arrived home, a bouquet of long-stemmed, deep purple roses—my favorite—from Eric were on my doorstep. My answering machine's light was blinking. The first call was from David Finkel. He wanted to see me. The second call was Eric's, telling me how much he adored me.

"I'll be down in two weeks, my precious," he promised. "Please be patient."

Patient, hell, I thought. The next day, I called Dr. Graham's office.

CHAPTER 6

I spoke to Susan Tyler, Dr. Graham's head nurse. When she asked the purpose of my wanting to come in, the words stuck in my throat, and I finally blurted out that I needed to have something done about the dark circles under my eyes and my droopy eyelids.

"A-also," I stammered, "I, uh, might decide to have some extra work done after I see Dr. Graham."

His first available appointment was two months away. My heart sank that I would have to wait for so long. "I'll take it, but if you have any cancellations, please call me. I can come in at any time."

I felt terrified and exuberant after making the phone call. Moving forward with my plan was my secret. The dream was becoming a reality. I dared to feel the full impact of my decision, and it shook me to the core. I felt alone.

Then I lifted my chin, pretended that I felt confident and powerful, and made myself believe it.

I went to my desk and found some of the notes I'd taken during my conversation with Susan at Braun's office. She had explained several procedures for reconstruction surgery, which creates a new breast. I remember our talking about how it can enhance the woman's self-concept. Of course, I had to realize that eighty percent of the women desiring the procedure can be candidates. Because of the complexity, candidates should contact only board-certified plastic surgeons like Braun Graham and the other doctors in his office.

Susan said that some women with newly diagnosed breast cancer want cooperation between their cancer surgeon and plastic surgeon, so when they awake from surgery, they have a new breast.

The most common method of breast reconstruction is a surgical implant or prosthesis, the second is the "tummy tuck" method, and the third, less often selected is the "Latissimus dorsi" approach, she had reminded me.

The surgical implant or prosthesis is inserted underneath the area where the breast would normally be located. The plastic surgeon creates a pocket beneath the skin and the remaining muscle. The prosthesis is either a thin, flexible plastic or silicone gel, saline solution, or combination of materials.

I had underlined information about the tummy tuck. It's a difficult undertaking for the patient because it involves both abdominal and breast surgery, and healing takes longer than for the simple implant. The reward is that the patient gets a trimmer figure. I had drawn a smile on my notes. The Latissimus dorsi approach is used when there is too little skin to accommodate the implant. Additional skin, muscles, and blood vessels from the woman's back are moved to her breast area to create a prosthesis and implant. Patients are left with a scar on the back.

Chemotherapy and radiation treatments may be continued after reconstruction surgery. Cooperation between the medical and radiation oncologist is essential to derive the best sequence of chemo- and radiation therapy.

I knew I was doing everything right. Braun Graham was board certified.

I thought about those women who arranged for a plastic surgeon to reconstruct a breast directly following the mastectomy, who awakened from the anesthesia with a breast. Had I been given that option, would I be a different woman today? There could be no answer to that question. All I knew was that I would be a different woman soon.

I celebrated eight years of surviving cancer by hosting a party. Even though money was tight and I would need every penny for my operation in January, I felt the need to have my friends and family around to celebrate the grand occasion. I had napkins printed with "Happiness is . . . surviving 8 years."

Marc, Joel, and Sara flew down to join the sixty

other guests. I invited David. He and I had seen each other a few times since I came back from Wisconsin.

The catered food included chicken with peanut sauce, shrimp, pasta salad, roasted nuts, Brie with fruit and cognac, marinated tenderloin with small homemade rolls, and trays of pastries, including cookies with the number eight.

Unfortunately Eric was not able to get away, but he sent me a huge bouquet of purple roses in a crystal vase and a very generous check to help defray the cost of the festivities.

As I began my ninth year of life after cancer, I knew I was going to bloom, and there would be new leaves on my purple tree. I was moving into a new phase of life, a time of wellness inside a new and perfect body.

David came late, toward the end of the party. He said that he had fallen asleep without setting his alarm clock. I was annoyed.

I was spending time with him because part of my nurturing personality sympathized with his problems. We would end up cooking dinner together, then playing Cribbage. We'd each put a quarter in a jar after every game and use the money for a night out.

After a month of this, finally, I decided not to continue with our relationship.

Before Marc, Joel, and Sara left for Minnesota and

Missouri, we walked the beach. Again, I shared my feelings about reconstruction surgery. They thought that my surgery wasn't necessary, that I was fine with one breast and dark circles under my eyes. So my eyelids drooped and were swollen—big deal. "You're just going through a depression because things aren't working out for you and Eric or David," they told me.

I turned on them. I could feel the fire blazing from my eyes as I glared at them. I struggled to keep my voice from shaking.

"It is not because of Eric or David, although I want to attract a healthier man. More important, I want control of my life. I want to become a patient, not a victim. I want to look well. I'm putting that part of my life behind me. This change is essential to my survival. This surgery is a statement to myself and the universe that I'm not going to get cancer again. I must start being this new woman—now."

They looked at me with uncertainty. I felt devastated that we hadn't reached a reconciliation before they had to go home. I felt completely at peace with my decision. I began healing.

I called Dr. Graham's office the next morning to confirm our appointment. Then I took a deep breath and said, "Susan, I'm coming in to discuss reconstructive surgery."

"That makes a difference in how we schedule your consultation. Are you sure about this?"

"Very."

"Thanks for letting us know. You're all set, then. Reconstruction consultation it is. We'll see you on Wednesday."

Dressing for my appointment with Dr. Graham, I felt some apprehension about whether or not he would consider me a good candidate for surgery. I was also worried about his reaction to my malpractice suit. I was sure Susan had told him about it.

As I walked into Graham's office, then his examining room, my eyes took in the whole, wonderful environment—part of my training as an interior designer. The soft recessed lighting gave off a feeling of warmth. The paintings were of two beautiful women. On one wall was a blackboard; on another were two framed certificates—one from the Harry J. Buncke Society, for continued innovation and excellence in microvascular surgery, dated 1985; the other had to do with Graham's fellowship at the Microsurgical Unit of Ralph K. Davies Medical Center—and a photograph of two doctors performing surgery.

A comfortable chair sat in the corner, and a stool was next to the examining table. I changed from my clothes into my white satin boa. I felt good about wearing it.

When Dr. Graham walked in, his warm, amused smile allayed my fears.

My words came in a rush. "I want reconstructive surgery." Then I told him my medical history.

"Whose decision is it to have the surgery, Diane?" he asked. "Is anyone pressuring you into it?"

I laughed. "No-o-o. It's mine alone," I answered strongly.

He asked me to tell him about my boa. He loved that I had worn it for my chemo and radiation appointments, to keep my morale high.

Dr. Graham explained that because my skin was so radiated, the only reconstructive surgery he would perform on me would be the procedure called a *Tram Flap*.

I wasn't familiar with this method. Dr. Graham explained that it involves moving skin and fat from the lower abdomen below the mastectomy site to the breast area. One advantage is the good skin match in color and texture between the breast and the belly.

He would make a flap of muscle, skin, and tissue from my abdominal region, and that flap would be tunneled under the skin to the mastectomy site. Once in place, it creates the breast mound. I'd end up with a horizontal scar across my lower abdomen. A nipple and areola would be added later from another part of my body.

"How strong is your commitment?" he asked.

"Very."

"Good, because you'll need it. This will be a four-stage process that will take close to a year to complete."

He drew a diagram on the blackboard, showing me exactly what he would accomplish. He agreed that after the reconstruction was completed on my right breast, the left breast would be too heavy and large, an unsightly reminder of the past. Because the left breast strained my back, neck, and shoulder, he would perform a breast-reduction so the two sides would match.

I was very excited. "When can we schedule the surgery? How about tomorrow?"

Graham chuckled. "Not quite, but soon." He called the front desk and asked them to coordinate his schedule and the hospital's. They came back with a Thursday that was only three weeks away. He never performed surgery on Thursdays but was making an exception for me. I reached out and hugged him, then we shook hands.

"Let's go for it!" I said. "Let's just go for it!"

CHAPTER 7

The reason why a patient undergoes so many emotional as well as physical changes during the initial period of cancer discovery and therapy is that life changes totally after the doctor says, "You have cancer." The patient's world is turned upside down. She can continue to be healthy in the Cancer World, but she can never again cross into the Well World.

I wrote those words in the article about prostate- and breast-cancer patients. Now I was challenging my own beliefs by trying to move into that "forbidden" world where only healthy people reside.

I was not the only one to believe it was a place I would never again inhabit. When I sued Dr. Jackson, one of my expert witnesses had been Dr. Harvey Golomb, director of the Joint Section on Hematology-Oncology at the University of Chicago Medical Center and Michael Reese Medical Center. A full professor of medicine at the University of Chicago, he had written and published 216 articles and texts. When asked in court to comment about my life expectancy, his answer terrified me. He began by remarking on the significance of my second breast lump:

> We usually understand that this is the tip of the iceberg. . . . I think she'll have evidence of systemic relapse probably within the next year or two. I think the major message to understand is that once the disease recurs, the patient will never be cured. . . . Since it has recurred, she's going to have continual problems with this and will eventually die of cancer. . . .

I had beaten the odds and the experts' predictions by surviving two bouts with a malignancy. Now I had the audacity to want more favors from God. It was an exhilarating and bold prospect.

While thinking about my future, I began to focus on my dysfunctional affairs with David and Eric. I wondered what those liaisons implied about me. Sure, having two fellows in my life gave me something to think about besides myself and my cancer, and I loved being in a man's company. But I suddenly knew I had to leave both lovers behind. Precious little was right and good about either relationship. The answer came to me in a moment of horrible clarity: I put more value on their accepting me with only one breast than on anything else about them. It was difficult for me to accept that I had made such unacceptable choices, but they represented what was wrong with my self-image. I had seen myself as a charity case. I had to expunge my feelings of being a victim.

Soon, having one breast was going to be part of my past. I would be leaving my cancer chest and the wrong men behind. I would be making room for a long-term, positive, healthy, loving relationship.

Breaking up with either man wouldn't be easy for me. Eric was everything I had ever wanted in a mate. And whenever he sensed my loneliness and dissatisfaction, he would visit me as soon as he could get away. He repeated how much he wanted to grow old with me. He seemed so much in love with me.

He always had a way to convince me of his sincerity and his plans for our future together. I would sell my condo on the beach and move into a place that would be ours together. He wanted to meet my boys and daughter-in-law.

And Eric was generous with gifts and money. I always appreciated his help.

As for David, I would need someone to give me a hand when I got out of the hospital. For all of his faults, he liked feeling needed, and I knew I could count on his assistance. He also had a keen sense of humor.

The final battle was against my own fear. If I had two breasts and persisted in going out with the wrong kind of man, I wouldn't have any excuses.

Now that I had a date for surgery, I was ready to tell the world. I felt like dancing around my living room. Some of my anger and self-hatred vanished. My life took on a party atmosphere. I began to visualize myself as a two-breasted woman with a zest for life. I would wear elegant bras with matching panties. I would buy a two-piece bathing suit.

I made a commitment to be more frugal because I would be living a long life. I looked forward to finding an unmarried man who would want to spend his life with me. I became reconciled—no, eager—to spend time alone until a companion who understood me and would be good to me entered my life.

I promised myself to exercise regularly.

I called Aetna to alert them of the fax transmission that Dr. Graham's office would be sending later in the week. He would have to receive from them a certificate of agreement before we went ahead with the surgery.

I wanted Aetna's verbal agreement immediately, and I got it. Now I was ready to tell the world!

I called my dear Aunt Nish and my Uncle George. They, along with Marc, Joel, and my former father-in-law, are the lasting rewards from my marriage. Uncle George was an anesthesiologist and chief of staff at St. Mary's Hospital in Knoxville, Tennessee. He and Aunt

Nish listened, then offered their unconditional support. George asked if I understood the seriousness of the surgery. I didn't consider that I was taking a risk; to me, I didn't have a choice.

I also called Gladys and Milt, friends I had met through Nish and George. Gladys has been like an older sister to me. They, too, expressed their enthusiasm and offered help.

Next I contacted Dr. Carbone to let him know of my decision. He wished me luck. He was more aware now how important this surgery had become to me.

"It isn't elective anymore, Paul. It's a matter of my survival."

He understood. "I'll speak with Dr. Graham. Please make sure I'm kept informed of your progress. Good luck. And most of all, Diane, be well."

Then I spoke to Isaac Levine, my medical oncologist in Naples, Florida. He was Dr. Carbone's protege at UWCCC and had been assigned to my case in 1984, while I was still living in Madison. He always encouraged me to have reconstruction surgery. Now he wished me the best and, like Paul, wanted Braun to call him with progress reports. "You're doing the right thing, Diane," he said. "Good luck!"

Finally I called Marc and Joel. I wrote them each a letter about my plans, in which I accepted full responsibility for my life and decisions. I knew we would talk before they received the letters.

I jumped another hurdle in my life by taking control and moving forward. I had a new horizon, and my path had no footsteps to follow. I'd make my own. Whoever Diane would become, the old one was disappearing.

CHAPTER 8

I knew I could not be alone when the bandages came off. I asked Sandy, my chemotherapy nurse, to stay with me. I closed my eyes until John, my surgeon, had removed the bandages completely. He said, "It looks terrific!"

I opened my eyes. He was smiling proudly. I forced myself to look down at my chest. Staples held my incision together. My chest was red. It hurt and was raw. I had no nipple. Only a few days before, I had had surgery. My breast was gone. I had a flat chest that had to heal along with my entire being. I suspected that my chest would heal faster than my emotions would.

My surgeon told me that all the redness would disappear eventually. The drains and tubes would be taken out shortly. My upper chest wall was not indented. John had left as much flesh as he could, so I would still have a cleavage. John said that once I had healed, my incision would be very thin and *not noticeable.* I laughed at him, although tears fell on my cheeks. Of course it was going to be noticed!

After Sandy and John left me alone in the hospital room, I gently explored the new incision and touched my flat chest. I felt my left breast and my nipple. I held my hand on my breast for a few moments. Then I slid my fingertips to my flat breast. It was sore, with an uneven feeling around the incision. I looked down in silence. I was lopsided. The area where my right breast had been now looked like a circle bisected horizontally with a puffy top and bottom and a straight line across the center, which extended from my chest into my underarm.

Shaking my head in disbelief, I felt tears roll over my face. If losing one breast or both would save my life, it was a small price to pay.

I put down the typewritten pages that described the moment a little more than eight years before when I saw my breastless chest for the first time. I shook my head at the words *not noticeable.* John hadn't meant to be insensitive or to minimize my loss. He was a wonderful, caring surgeon. But he just didn't—and maybe, because he was a man, couldn't—understand what a woman's breasts mean to her.

A woman's breasts have long been associated with her sexuality. Age is not an issue here. It is ridiculous to assume that breasts don't matter to women in midlife and beyond. A woman's need for a positive self-image isn't cut away with her tumor and breast tissue. Whether young, middle-aged, or old, cancer patients have wildly fluctuating self-images caused, in part, by the alterations that affect their body. Ideally patients learn to live with, accept, and adjust to the changes. But all that takes time . . . if it happens at all.

While I was scheduling myself for reconstruction, Dr. David Kessler, chairman of the Food and Drug Administration, banned silicone breast implants. Defective implants had leaked gel and created health problems for women. People were talking about how unnecessary reconstructive surgery was and how sad it was that young women had endangered their health for the sake of "vanity." I knew, however, from the correspondence I received from readers of *Journey* and from talking with so many people, including physicians, that most women disagreed. For them, reconstruction was necessary.

I believed that our society's preoccupation with breast size was partly responsible for sending young women to plastic surgeons for augmentation or reconstruction. The issue is much more complex and primal, perhaps even part of females' collective unconscious and having to do with motherhood. It represents one generation's gift to the next because a mother's breasts nourish her young. God gave us breasts for many reasons, not just for reasons of sexuality or to attract a bedmate. My new mission, I decided, might be to enlighten others with my hard-won awareness that there is nothing like a breast.

Dr. Graham's preference was to use my own blood during the surgery. This would protect me from any problems caused by using someone else's. His office arranged to have a pint taken from me at two different appointments, one week apart. He planned to infuse my stored blood to "supercharge" the circulation to my new breast, and that would speed my recovery. Before my blood was taken, I had to sign for permission to be tested for AIDS and Hepatitis B.

Dr. Graham faxed his proposal, including expenses, to the Aetna Insurance Company. Breast reconstruction is covered by most reputable insurance companies because they do not consider it to be cosmetic surgery.

Aetna has proven itself to be a fine and honorable company, and it occupies a special place in my heart. Because of the completeness of the questions in their forms and how Dr. Jackson answered them ten years ago after my office visits, they were used as powerful evidence against him during my lawsuit.

Aetna promptly sent back written approval to Dr. Graham. The company agreed to pay most of the medical expenses. I wanted a private room and was willing to pay the difference between that and a semiprivate room, which Aetna would cover.

Dr. Graham's office gave me a list of Patient's Responsibilities. I planned to follow every detail; I didn't want to make any mistakes. I would be in Sarasota Memorial for five days. After I was discharged, I couldn't lift anything or vacuum my condo. I wouldn't be able to walk the beach or travel beyond Sarasota or drive for three weeks. No problem—friends volunteered to chauffeur me around.

I was to take extra Tamoxifen for two days and none on the day of surgery. Then, the day after my operation, I would go back to my regular schedule of two pills a day. I had to have a chest X ray and mammogram before surgery.

I made sure I had a good supply of Extra Strength Tylenol. I stashed money in the house for emergencies.

The cupboards were full. Chicken breasts were in the freezer, along with quarts of chicken soup and matzo balls. Many friends offered to bring casseroles to me. I had fresh oranges and grapefruit for juice, and the liquor cabinet was stocked with wine, vodka, and scotch.

I joined Sarasota Memorial's Century Club. After

all, I contributed so much money to the University of Wisconsin Comprehensive Cancer Center, I felt it was only fair to be a donor to my new hospital.

I had to have someone with me my first night home from the hospital. I asked David to stay with me, and he agreed, as I knew he would. In fact, he offered to stay with me for a few days. He volunteered to prepare some meals. I accepted with alacrity; he was a good cook, and he was fun. His pitching in helped him to feel important. Before my operation, David was supportive. One evening while we were playing Cribbage, he expressed concern that I was undergoing the reconstruction so that he would be more attracted to me.

"Absolutely not!" I told him. "I'm doing it for myself, not for any man."

After Marc and Joel received my letter, they called and told me all they wanted was for me to be happy and healthy. I loved them so much.

They asked about coming to Sarasota, but I told them to wait until I had recuperated.

During Eric's daily phone calls, he assured me that he would be part of my new life with my new body. It was impossible not to believe him; everything in my life took on a rosy glow.

He would be the first lover to embrace my new breast. I felt like a virgin again. I wouldn't be able to have sex for two weeks, but that wouldn't be a hardship because Eric wasn't scheduled to come south for another month. In the meantime, he sent me a check to defray some of my medical expenses.

I started to rely on his generosity each month. Eric knew my living expenses were much more than I earned, so he volunteered his assistance. At first I refused; I was too proud to take his money. Then Eric explained that his contribution was a substitute for his physical presence whenever he wasn't able to help in person. As our relationship deepened and promises were made for our future together, I relented with gladness and relief.

The night before my surgery, I walked the beach at sunset. I sat under my purple tree and happily watched buds appear, ready to unfurl as my new beginning took shape.

I prayed that all would go well for me the next day and forever, and I felt confident that it would. I had listened to my inner guidance all along and every step of the way kept my heart and mind in alignment.

That evening I showered with the special soap Dr. Graham had given me. It was the last time I had to touch my mastectomy scar. As I watched the suds go down the drain, I felt as if I were washing away the past eight years and scouring away Bob Jackson's influence on my life.

CHAPTER 9

I got up early; earlier than Uncle George's wake-up reminder call at five in the morning. He was kidding, of course.

As I was dressing, I stopped and stared in the mirror. This is the last time I'll have this figure, I thought. I'm going to have two beautiful breasts again.

Those words had become a mantra, affirming my health and longevity. I'm growing old with two breasts.

The phone didn't stop ringing—the boys called to say good luck, then Eric wished me well. He said he would talk to Braun later, and if he could, he would speak to me. I felt frustrated that he wasn't with me but was grateful for his unflagging support.

I was ready when George and Nish came to pick me up at five thirty and euphoric during the ride to the hospital. I asked George to join me in the preoperative room. While he kept me company, he and my anesthesiologist made small talk and realized that they knew many of the same physicians from Wisconsin and

Tennessee. This was a good omen! I felt protected by how George and Eric were acting as liaisons for me with other members of the medical profession.

My nurse had problems starting the IV; the veins on my left arm were still weakened from chemotherapy. My anesthesiologist took over, and after two attempts, he succeeded. My right arm had been coded red—it could not be used for any procedures—because my lymph nodes had been removed during my mastectomy.

George gave me a kiss and wished me luck as the staff rolled me into the operating room. Braun, wearing a big smile, came over to me.

"Are you ready?" he asked.

"You better believe it," I answered. "Let's go! Thumbs up!"

Braun came in the next morning. Grinning, he asked if I had seen my breast or touched it yet.

"No," I told him. "I wanted to wait until you were with me."

He took off some tape, and I looked down. "Go ahead," he urged. "Touch it."

I did. It was soft yet firm, even with tape around the incision. After eight years, I was able to look down and see cleavage. The breath caught in my throat.

"It's yours forever, Diane," he said softly.

Tears of joy welled up in my eyes. "Thank you," I whispered. My surgery had taken seven and a half hours. There was more scar tissue from the radiation therapy than Braun had anticipated. He had to tie off each blood vessel so I wouldn't bleed excessively.

After he left my room, the nurses helped me with my tubes and drains. My lower abdomen had two tubes, one on each side, as well as on the side of my breast. I had a catheter because I wasn't supposed to move. The IV was in my left arm, and a machine allowed me to administer my own pain medicine whenever I needed it.

As soon as I was alone, my hands roamed over the new addition to my body. I felt so happy and so good about myself! No doubt my positive vibes would keep my immune system producing antibodies that would keep me well!

Gladys and Milt had been in my room when I was wheeled up from Recovery, and Gladys kept her promise to be holding my hand when I awakened.

Now other visitors came, and my excitement bubbled up with every new person. "I did it!" I said as each guest came in the door. "I actually did it!"

After my mastectomy, my flat chest became a symbol of my courage but also of death. Now my rounded breast was a symbol of life.

This operation is not for everyone. It won't replace

the implant surgery for many patients. The *Tram Flap* is more complicated and more costly than other procedures. But in my opinion, it's worth it.

David visited me and brought me flowers. He kissed me hello on my cheek. He settled into a chair and watched television, or we played Cribbage. I watched him from the corner of my eye and regretted our friendship's ups and downs.

Why, I wondered, thinking about David and Eric, are people so reluctant to change?

Even with the gauze around the incisions and the drains, I was able to sense my changing. All I had to do was look down at this gorgeous mound of flesh. Mine.

Sometimes I remembered how sweet the weeks had been when David was courting me. How might our relationship be different, I wondered, if we were to make love after my reconstruction?

I asked David to touch my new breast. He did, reluctantly.

Before I went home from the hospital, Braun told me that he had ordered a biopsy of tissue around my chest wall and stomach. All the tests had come back negative. Free of cancer, I breathed easier and felt fortunate to have such a thorough doctor.

I got dressed carefully. I still had a drain on the side of my breast and two in my abdomen. They would stay in for another week, until the fluid was gone. This didn't detract from the joy I felt whenever I looked at myself. My high right breast looked quite different from the low-slung left one. The scars of the past were gone. Now I had beautiful new incisions. Learning to live without cancer was proving to be a lot easier than learning to live with it.

Uncle George drove me home. David made dinner the first evening. I talked with the boys every day. Eric called many times each day during the week. I rested as much as possible.

A week later, I had an appointment with Braun. He removed the drains and changed the tape around my incisions. He was as delighted and proud of his artistry as I was to be its owner.

I treated David to dinner on my first night out to thank him for his generous caring. He was warm and loving toward me at the restaurant. Because he had an early morning appointment, we went home shortly after we finished dinner. He gave me a gentleman's kiss good-night at the door.

I was alone with my thoughts. I undressed and stared in the mirror at my new chest. Then I closed my eyes and wished Eric could have been with me.

My wish came true soon enough. I picked him up at the airport. His eyes dancing, he kissed me every time I stopped the car at a red light. The anticipation of making love was nearly all consuming. I felt so sexy; it was like being an adolescent again.

Once inside "our" home, we kissed passionately. I had bought two silk bras and matching panties. I had so much fun going into Victoria's Secret and selecting what I thought of as "fantasy" bras.

Eric quickly pulled my shirt over my head and flung it across the room, then looked at me. He grinned. "It's beautiful, like you." He bent to kiss my new breast. "Braun is an artist."

I stood weak-kneed. "Our new playmate," he murmured into my cleavage, and his hands were soft and gentle. He undressed quickly. "I love you, Diane," he whispered. "I think about our being together."

Our lovemaking was intense. I felt free. My self-consciousness was gone. No longer did I try to hide my scarred, barren chest. Taking in the sight of my new, thin body, we touched my new breast. With our new play toy, I learned that Eric definitely was a breast man. And now, I was his breast lady.

Eric took Braun and his wife, Jeanne, out to a gourmet restaurant for dinner. It was his way of thanking Braun for taking such good care of me and to show his respect for Braun's brilliance as a surgeon. Eric said that Braun was one of those wonderful human beings and fine doctors whom we are lucky to find in life.

Eric asked Braun's advice about his relocating to Sarasota or Naples from Madison. He said that he was gathering information about taking the Florida boards in order to practice after his move. Braun encouraged him to come down. My heart swelled as I listened. I glowed with happiness to hear him speaking in such concrete terms in front of my surgeon. My lover was taking concrete steps at last!

During dinner, Eric couldn't stop looking at me. I wore a white silk shirt with a low neckline. We went home and made more love. We hardly got out of bed the entire weekend.

It was so tough for us to say good-bye on Sunday afternoon, Eric made plans to come back again within the month, even though he'd be able to get away for only twenty-four hours. He didn't want to be away for so long, he said. He wanted to see "our child" and fondle it.

I reminded him it was my breast. It belonged to me. It was feeling more like a permanent part of my life.

As I drove him to the airport, I pressed him for a specific timetable. When was he coming down for good?

He asked for a little more time. He needed to lay groundwork for a career in Florida, he said. But I wasn't appeased. For the first time in almost a decade, I didn't have to settle for less than exactly what I wanted and needed.

CHAPTER 10

Six Months Later

I was the happiest I'd been in a long time. As I sat under my purple tree on the beach, I looked up and admired the strong limbs that had appeared recently. Although moving to Sarasota had been a superb decision, opting for reconstruction surgery surpassed it. My breast gave me an added dimension; I felt sweet, soft, and gentle. I felt beautiful. I felt satisfied. I loved what I saw in the mirror. There's nothing like my breast.

I couldn't have anticipated the depth of my feeling of freedom—a manifestation of the wellness inside my body and soul. My new gentleness in my body cut away the violence of my cancer.

I became less lonely, more self-sufficient. Eric had invited me to meet him in Chicago for a few days, and I refused. Even after all this time, even with the benefit of watching how positive change can be, he was still not with me.

I shaded my eyes and looked toward the west. As the tropical sun lowered over Siesta Beach, the more orange and unreal it appeared. A deep golden glow washed over the gulfside condominiums, and the beachwalkers' shadows lengthened. For a while the sun hung in the sky, seemingly unmoving. Sometimes I had felt like that, in limbo. After my surgery, though, I experienced more control over my life. I enjoyed greater emotional strength.

I needed fortitude to weather a disappointment: An award-winning producer for television miniseries wanted to option *Journey*, with the intention of bringing it to television or the movies. But he and my attorney in New York had been unable to agree on terms. I'd received hundreds of letters over the years from women thanking me for *Journey*. Now I felt regret that the thousands who might benefit from seeing my story on television or in theaters wouldn't have the opportunity. Not yet, Diane, I told myself, looking up through the indigo leaves. Someone will produce it someday.

While I had that thought, the sun plunged into the water and threw an afterglow across the deepening darkness of the sky. The way the sun hit the water, it looked like a big round boob. I laughed. I had breasts on my mind.

My second surgery, the reduction of my left breast, was scheduled for the next morning. Besides reducing its size, Braun planned to tighten the skin beneath it, lifting it so it would be on the same level as my new one. His intention while raising the nipple was to keep all the nerves in it.

At the same time, my eyes, both upper and lower lids, would finally be tightened.

I was eager to have the second procedure completed. My breast reduction would give me a different look. My eyes would look brighter.

How drastically perceptions can change! I thought as I undressed in my bathroom. For years I had been so grateful for my large and healthy left breast. Now it felt unmanageable.

I stepped into the shower and lathered with the special soap, feeling like a veteran at this familiar procedure.

When I awoke after my surgery, Aunt Nish was with me. I looked down. My breast felt lighter and was round and perfect. I couldn't keep my hands off my breasts.

Braun came in and reported that he had checked all of my tissue before completing his surgery and everything was negative. Thank God. Saving my life is the only thing that matters.

I wished the boys had been there to hold my hand and share my joy.

My eyes were sore, black and blue, and swollen. Braun instructed me to alternate hot and cold compresses on them. The fatty excess was removed and the upper lids were tightened. The cyst was removed. The dark circles and swelling under my eyes will be gone once I'm healed.

I remember the difficulty I had with my eyes after I lost my eyelashes from chemotherapy, during my first bout with breast cancer. Some of the medicine blurred my eyesight. The doctors thought I might have a more serious problem, such as glaucoma. After I was finished with chemo, however, my eyes went back to normal. My eyelashes grew back scant, but I was grateful for them. Oddly, my eyebrows became thicker.

As I got dressed to go home, I looked down at my new, symmetrical torso. This view had been lost to me for so long. I felt like the bionic woman—no, even better, I felt as if my body and soul were finally united.

David called to acknowledge my birthday. Because his and mine are a week apart, we went out to dinner to celebrate. He had kept in touch over the months between my surgeries, but I hadn't encouraged our getting together.

Eric came down the weekend after my birthday. Ostensibly, he was in Florida for a medical conference he needed to attend, and he did spend some of his time there. But he also made time for me. Because we had three days together, we had time to love, take walks, and visit with my friends, who all accepted him as my lover and future husband.

Before Eric left, he asked me not to see any other men. I told him I would think about it. I didn't think it was fair for him to expect exclusivity. I needed companionship, too. I wanted a man who cherished me. Eric assured me that he was that man and that I had achieved my dreams.

I sensed that Eric was feeling threatened by my new looks even though I wasn't dating anyone else. If I had met a man who could give me what I wanted and needed, I probably would have handed my lover a deadline for marrying me. I worked hard not to commit my love to him. After enjoying wonderful, leisurely days together, his leaving was particularly wrenching. Our affair gave me tremendous joy, but I suffered from it, also.

Just before Eric's visit, I had attended a wedding and wept throughout the sermon. I gazed out the church window while the minister spoke about love, commitment, and God, and about two people struggling and growing together. I wanted to share all that with Eric. He had called, sensing my blue mood, to pledge his heart to me. But I knew full well, then and now, he was not mine. It was, I admitted with heartbreaking sorrow, time for another change in my life, and it had to do with Eric. Do I have the strength to do what needs to be done?

I wondered. Before, I had been too weak to do more than make ineffectual demands on him. Now my self-esteem was growing. I felt freer, more confident about my attractiveness and optimistic about the future. These new attitudes would have to spill over onto my love affair. But he was a lot to give up.

Throwing off my cancer-victim mentality had been a primary motivation for reconstruction. Now my role as the mistress-victim was becoming uncomfortably clear to me. In spite of the sacrifices I'd have to make, I knew I would be making a change soon, whether Eric liked it or not.

It was time for some "consumer therapy" to raise my spirits. I bought most of my clothes at the Foxy Lady Boutique. Lorry, the owner, had become a friend of mine over the past three years. The boutique's clothes are very feminine and avant garde. For years I had looked longingly at their fashion racks, but I hadn't bought many of the styles because of my shape and prosthesis. There was something slightly masochistic about my visits to Foxy Lady, a place to grieve my precancer body.

I hadn't worn a tank top for years because I needed my bodices loose enough to shield my prosthesis and large breast. I wore elastic-waisted full skirts because they were less revealing than slacks. Jackets were important so I could hide my stomach and hips. Now all that had changed. I went with Gladys to buy my first two-piece bathing suit in nine years.

Lorry was in the store when we walked in. I asked her to help me find my dream-come-true two-piece bathing suit. No more black, old-fashioned swimsuits! I told her. She carried in armloads of suits to try. Everyone in the store—saleswomen and customers alike—shared my excitement as word of my quest spread. Lorry finally found the perfect swimsuit for me: The fabric had red hibiscus flowers and green leaves on a navy background.

I hugged Gladys and Lorry. I was jumping up and down like a little child. I knew that in spite of everything I had gone through over the years, this moment, with my new two-piece bathing suit, was God's reward for me.

I also picked out a one-piece swimsuit that, unlike my other garments that had to accommodate the prosthesis, didn't have a definite cup. Gathered tightly around my stomach, the suit was bright red and fuchsia.

My world where I was so angry and uncomfortable seemed very far away. The day when I had thrown down my prosthesis seemed in the distant past.

God, I had waited a long time for this feeling! I looked down and saw the fruits of surviving. My breasts were gorgeous. Perfect! This was Diane! It was my miracle. I could hardly believe where I had been these past years.

CHAPTER 11

I am aware that some people will be incensed because I'm giving breasts so much importance in my life. My critics, however, may not have lived eight years without one. *Penthouse* and *Playboy* magazines are merely saying and showing what is true: Breasts are important. Otherwise, why would women bother to wear an uncomfortable prosthesis?

Our physiological makeup allows both men and women to enjoy the pleasurable sensitivity of breasts. Men like to have their nipples and breasts caressed and sucked as much as women do. Breasts are the only "sexual equipment" men and women share. I think men like to experience sensual pleasure from their breasts and nipples as a way to share what women feel.

Sadly, men, too, are victims of breast cancer. They now comprise about seven-tenths of a percent of the cases, and the trend is on the rise.

But the importance of our breasts must be kept in

perspective. I still become upset with women who say they wouldn't have had their mastectomy if reconstructive surgery weren't available. My mastectomy saved my life. I would never have martyred myself just to keep my breast.

Eric and I talked often about the fact that I had no treatment options; I had to lose my breast and lymph nodes. As a physician, he believed in taking the least traumatic action—a lumpectomy and radiation. He believed in conserving the breast if at all possible. He liked to discuss his work, and until I had my second surgery, I was a willing listener. I found it interesting to hear about the breast cancer he had been dealing with and his research.

Many of our conversations concluded with his hashing over Bob Jackson's misdiagnosis. At first, talking about it was an ordeal—I did not want to relive the nightmare. Then, after my second surgery, the topic became entirely irrelevant to my new life, and I was bored by it. I found myself changing the topic.

Discussing cancer with Eric seemed so negative! I wanted to talk about our feelings, our relationship, our spirituality, the movies, current events. I wanted to talk about life! Is illness a common issue of such magnitude that our closeness will suffer without it? I wondered.

Aunt Nish and I drove to Naples, Florida, to have my examination with Isaac Levine. My heart beat quickly, and my blood pressure was up. I was very nervous, in spite of the wonderful reports Braun had gotten back after my surgery. Even though all the biopsies had been negative, Isaac looked for other symptoms.

Isaac is one of the "privileged few." This is a concept I devised nearly forty years ago, when I became aware of the differences between optimistic, creative people who live consciously and are in touch with their feelings and the rest of the population, which bumble and lumber through life. One of the most important characteristics of the privileged few is their fearless risk-taking and changing the course of their life into new directions.

Because the privileged few focus only on the positive, they don't waste precious time in untenable circumstances. They constantly readjust their situation to what's right for them and their loved ones. Isaac, for example, left Wisconsin and moved to Florida. He resigned from a successful practice in Madison, but opened a new one in Naples and remarried. He is very happy with the changes he made.

Isaac had recently returned from Madison, where he saw Eric. "I've known that man for years, and he's never looked so good," Isaac told me. "He's had a special smile and a twinkle in his eye since he's been with you. I told him that, too. I said, "Eric, with Diane you've got everything.""

Isaac encouraged him to come down to Florida. "I told him that his life would be filled with joy, just like mine is now with Shirley. You two have my blessings."

Next door to Isaac's office was an oncology center, and he had told Eric that a successful research lab was his for the asking.

I knew that Eric wanted to make the leap from his old life into a new one, but I wasn't sure he had the courage, even when we talked about our goals. He frequently discussed changing careers and leaving medicine. In truth, Eric didn't know what he wanted. I was afraid that until all the puzzle pieces were in place for him, he'd be paralyzed.

His parents had sent him away to a private school so he would be with the "right" people. They wanted him to go to medical school, and he succumbed to their demand. First he became a researcher and earned his Ph.D. Then he become a medical doctor. Sometimes the wonderful sound of his laughter stops when he puts on his white doctor's coat.

Together, we felt secure. However, when he went back to his other life, he accepted his fate. Could this man ever strike out on his own? I wondered. Would Eric ever be one of the privileged few?

I grew increasingly discontented with his inaction as I became totally honest with myself and pursued my dreams. Ironically, he encouraged me to be a free spirit.

He took delight in assisting me, probably because his independent impulses had always been crushed. I felt exasperated with our relationship. Unless he could make his own jump, he would be relegated to my past as I continued to move forward.

The issue of his infidelity concerned me. I told myself that if he had a new life with me, maybe he wouldn't need to cheat anymore. He claimed to be happy when he was with me.

Even though my eyes were black and blue from surgery, I went to a cocktail party. I figured if I could walk around bald for a year during my chemotherapy, I certainly could go to a cocktail party and wear a pair of sunglasses. The hosts were Kelly and Stella George, chairmen of our local Charting Committee of the Sarasota Power Squadron.

I joined the squadron because of my love for the water. The organization is a unit of the United States Power Squadrons—private, nonprofit, nongovernmental, nonmilitary, and open to both men and woman. Usually, their members love boating, and one of their goals is to promote boat safety.

The Charting Committee is a volunteer group that meets six times a year and looks for discrepancies between actual conditions and what is shown on the nautical charts. The reporter sends the findings to the United States

National Oceanic Atmospheric Administration. It's a tedious job, but someone's got to do it. . . .

After the charting work is done, the volunteers have lunch at one of the restaurants on the Intercoastal Waterway.

As I was leaving the party, I went to talk with an instructor in Seamanship. He introduced me to another couple and an older, pleasant-looking fellow named Saul Harris. I felt an attraction for him when he smiled.

When my instructor excused himself, Saul and I continued our conversation.

"Where's your husband?" he asked, looking around.

"I don't know," I answered. "I haven't seen him for years."

"Then you're single?"

I said yes.

He perked up and straightened his shirt. He told me that he was a widower. "Would you like to go out for coffee sometime?"

"That would be nice," I told him.

"How about dinner tonight?"

I blinked. The hosts had put on an elaborate buffet. "I'm not hungry."

"That's okay. Just sit with me while I eat. You can order something and take it home for breakfast."

I laughed. "That's an offer I can't refuse."

He followed me to my house, where I left my car. Then I drove with him to the restaurant.

"Why are you wearing sunglasses?" he asked.

"I had work done on my eyes."

He nodded and asked no more.

How nice, I thought, not having to worry about my mastectomy. With a shock I realized how early in a relationship my anxieties about my body used to set in, well before any possibility of a sexual relationship presented itself.

We talked for hours. He told me about his personal life. Sometimes, he told a joke.

After dinner we walked on Siesta Beach. It was a romantic night, with the moon shining on the water and the waves playing music.

I had a wonderful evening. We went back to my place for a cup of coffee. As we said good-night, he suddenly bent down and kissed me. Before kissing him back, I removed my glasses. "You look fine," he said.

"I have a boat," he added. "We could go out on it together. I'll call you soon. We'll set up a time."

I told him I'd like that, and knew that it would be nice.

CHAPTER 12

Summer was a time for traveling and visiting family. I went to Minnesota to see Joel and Sara. While I was there, I donated copies of *Journey* to libraries in Minneapolis and St. Paul. Everywhere I traveled, I took books to the local library and gave them as gifts.

Eric, wanting to meet my family, joined me for a few days. Madison to Minneapolis is a six-hour trip. He pulled into my son's driveway and bounded out of the car, as excited and happy as a child to see me.

I booked a room at a hotel not far from Joel and Sara's house. The kids joined us for dinner. Sara remarked later that we couldn't stop smiling and never stopped touching each other. To her, we looked desperately in love. Joel encouraged me to be patient until Eric could fully commit himself to a divorce.

Marc viewed Eric as a man who could be my equal and fly through life with me. He, like Joel, urged me to be patient. Patience, unfortunately, had never been one of my virtues.

Eric was open with the boys. He told them about his intention to grow old with me and about his love for me. He enjoyed Joel and Sara and Marc. They assured him his children would be welcomed into our family.

Eric and I had a wonderful vacation. One day, we went to the Walker Museum. On a rainy day we stayed inside and read and held hands. So companionable were we, Eric and I decided to see each other every three weeks.

But then, back in our hotel room, he would call home. Many times, he just invented a conference. I had heard the ruse many times, and sometimes I felt nauseated.

This time when he hung up, I told Eric that he couldn't call from our room anymore. Thereafter, he would excuse himself from the table after lunch or dinner and disappear toward the bank of public phones in the hotel lobby. I would wait for his return.

We drove back to Madison together in time for my six-month checkup with Paul Carbone. My friend Winona and her husband, Rolf, offered me their guest room. During my stay, I visited Ellie Anderson, my editor for *Journey to Justice*. Ellie had had breast cancer twice, the second occurrence five years after the first. She took one Tamoxifen a day (half my dosage) because she suffered an allergic reaction when she swallowed two. Now, after ten years of remission, she was battling another form of cancer.

I met Ellie in 1983, when she and Marc worked

together at National Public Radio in Madison. She visited me in the hospital after my mastectomy. Bless her, she told me how well she was doing with her cancers after all those years. I confided my fear and worry about what would happen to the boys if I died. The mother of four, Ellie had wrestled with the same emotions. I have never met anyone so empathetic before or since.

Ellie and I had become friends. Now I was afraid she was dying. I called her several times from Minneapolis and Madison, and her husband, Norman, told me she was too weak to talk. I asked if I could see her before I left for Florida, if only for five minutes. Norman told me to come right over.

I had to wear a special gown and a mask because Ellie was so vulnerable to infections. Tubes ran up and down her arm. I held on to her toe, the same way Joel had done for me during my chemo.

She smiled wanly. This was one time, she said in a quiet voice, when she wanted me to do all the talking. I told her about my trip to see Sara and Joel with Eric. I brought her up-to-date with *Journey* being in libraries across the country. I told her that, as editor, she was going to be famous. Ellie just asked me to spell her name correctly on the check, and I promised I would.

"I want to live," she told me. "It's the damned disease."

"You'll get out soon," I said with more conviction than I felt. "I'll call you after I get back home, and I'll visit you again before winter."

She nodded.

I wanted to do something, but I couldn't. I stood there helpless. I wanted to fight for her. I wanted to use whatever power I had to help her get well. I told her how I felt. "You have to get well!" I said, fighting back my tears. "We have so much to celebrate. After all, you have to dance at my wedding! You believe in miracles, don't you?"

She smiled. "I'll be there, but you and Eric better do it sooner rather than later."

"I'm working on it," I promised her.

My problems seemed miniscule as I watched her fade before my eyes. When I left, I kissed her feet under the covers, then blew her a kiss.

"Maybe you could visit me in Florida during your recuperation, Ellie."

She nodded and said she'd be down soon.

I told her how much I loved her, and she told me the same thing. I felt guilty. I was so alive.

Tears rolled down my cheeks. I didn't know if I would see her again.

Cancer is abusive and violent. Ironically, the treatments also do violence to the body. Yet, I would gladly undergo all the discomfort and misery of chemotherapy and radiation again to survive. Cancer is the body doing damage to itself, and the treatment has to be even more aggressive—otherwise you're fighting a brushfire that gets out of control. You must kill the cancer cells before they kill you, and you hope every mutating cell is being bombarded—I believe that's the only way to survive. As Paul once said to me, "You don't have a common cold; you have cancer."

While this destruction is going on, you are weathering physical and psychological changes. As you battle for life, you become selfish. The struggle for survival—both courageous and difficult—makes you beautiful in spite of the ravages of your body. You learn that outward beauty is merely that.

Naturally, life becomes more meaningful. You only want to surround yourself with positive people, events, and thoughts during your fight for life.

Now that I've won my fight against cancer, I laugh more. I appreciate participating in many different activities. I risk revealing my feelings, and I don't put things off for another time. I don't need to answer to anyone; my judgments are right for me. I feel liberated. I haven't felt this kind of peace for years.

The only thing I need is good health. Everything

else will follow. I feel God's presence every day. He has given me my life. It's hard to want anything more.

I was glad to be back in Sarasota. During my time in Madison, Eric behaved uncomfortably whenever we were together. He was worried about going places with me and being seen together in public. The fantasy of our love was gone. I felt disgusted with myself and wanted to call it quits. My new life of wellness created a more intense problem in our relationship. I was not willing to accept second best anymore. When I realized how precious my time is on this earth, I wondered why was I wasting it on Eric. I was tired of being alone. This is not the life I had fought for during these cancer years.

As soon as I walked in the door of my condo, the phone rang. It was Saul, asking me to go boating with him. I told him yes, even though I wouldn't have time to unpack.

He picked me up a short time later, and we attempted to go on a boat ride. Unfortunately, the low tide left us very little water. He asked me to give him a second chance when there was a higher tide.

I knew he was looking for romance, and I was very tempted. Seeing two men at the same time wasn't for me. I had to settle things with Eric one way or another, and soon. He had pledged to see me in three weeks, in

California. Then, as far as I was concerned, it was either go or no go.

I told Saul that I wanted him to be my friend and that sex wouldn't be appropriate now. Reluctantly, he agreed.

CHAPTER 13

I had my third procedure—an areola and nipple added to my new breast. As I lay on the table in one of his rooms designated for minor surgical precedures, Braun Graham removed skin from my right hip and grafted it onto my breast and created a nipple. He had to inject extra pain-killing shots into my breast. For some reason, I couldn't get numb; nerves had been growing into my previously numb breast.

As Braun and his head nurse, Susan, performed their artistry, we discussed the possibility of a book about my experiences with reconstruction. Braun reacted enthusiastically and thought it would be an important story for women and men to read.

"There!" Braun said, finished with the process. "This makes the breast a breast."

I agreed: I had loved my round breast before, but it didn't look like a breast until the nipple and areola were centered on it. Some women who have reconstruction never have the nipple replaced. To me, that would be like leaving the roof off a house. Before Braun and Susan put bandages on it, he showed me how beautiful it looked. I smiled. "This," I proclaimed, "is one beautiful breast!"

Braun told me not to swim for two weeks and to keep gauze on my nipple in case of some drainage.

I scheduled the appointment for my last procedure, three months away, when Susan would tattoo the color on my nipple and areola to match the natural side.

I was suffering separation anxiety, knowing that I had only one more procedure. My year-long commitment to the surgery had occupied my mind. Its completion reminded me of how I felt when I finished my chemotherapy and radiation series: I had been relieved I'd made it through but was lost without the security of my medical protocol.

My routine was going to change. I'd need to do something else. I'd be exploring my new psychological landscape. I planned to write about it.

In spite of my nervousness, I was thrilled to have an areola and nipple put on my breast after nine years without them. I felt very sexual. I looked down at my whole chest with two beautiful, healthy breasts.

I repeated to Braun that I didn't know how severe my unhappiness had been until I reached the heights of euphoria. I hadn't known how much I missed my breasts. I was Mrs. Well Adjusted, Mrs. Just Happy To Be Alive.

Mrs. Diane Craig "Who Needs a Breast, Anyway?" Chechik. Or so I had thought.

I urge every woman to have reconstruction if she's lost a breast. It isn't necessary to have the reconstruction done at the same time as the mastectomy. In fact, I believe there was an advantage to my waiting . . . although waiting so many years certainly isn't necessary. When you wait, you appreciate your reconstruction surgery more than if it's done immediately. Also, when you are breastless, the reality of your cancer cannot be denied. I believe that in order to heal, you must first deal with the fact of your illness.

Of course, there are advantages to having reconstruction during your mastectomy. Most obvious, you don't wake up without a breast, and that enhances your feelings of wellness. You have a more positive outlook on the future, knowing that all the cancer was excised. Clothes fit you immediately, and you don't have to bother with a prosthesis. Most of all, you feel like a patient, not a victim, of breast cancer.

I left Graham's office and drove home to pack. Later in the day I was meeting Eric in San Diego, where he had a medical convention. He did not know it yet, but he and I were headed for a showdown.

When I got off the airplane in California, Eric met me, and we kissed. He stood back, gripped my shoulders, and told me how much he loved me. Then we went down to get my luggage. He already had picked up his bags.

As we waited at the luggage carousel, he seemed jumpy. I knew he had a meeting in just a little while, and my suitcases had yet to appear.

"I'm leaving," he said at last.

"Fine. You go to your meeting. I'll take a cab to the hotel. I'll see you in the room later."

He laughed. "No, Diane, I'm leaving home. I want to live the rest of my life with you. Will you marry me, and spend the rest of your life with me?"

It took my breath away. I had waited more than a year to hear that declaration. "Yes!" I exclaimed, then advised him to get a divorce first, because bigamy is not accepted in most states. He agreed. We kissed in the midst of the airport crowd. "I reserved the hotel's honeymoon suite," he told me, his brown eyes sparkling.

When he left for his meeting, I warned myself to be cautious. As much as I loved this man, I felt uneasy. We had a long way to go.

I got changed and walked for hours around the harbor. I had a strange sense of separation from my surroundings, as if I were not in the real world. His proposal hadn't sunk in; otherwise, I would have been feeling happier. I glanced at my watch and saw it was time for me to meet him back at our suite.

When Eric returned, we jumped into bed and made love like two people who had just committed their lives to being together forever. We were one. When he kissed my breasts and carefully touched his tongue to my new nipple he looked up at me and said, "They love me, too. It's awesome, just awesome!"

My breasts were our new children of love. But I reminded him that they were mine, given to me by me as a token of the love I felt for myself. He only shared them.

He adored my new body and breasts. My nipple was still sore. When we finally rolled out of bed at dinnertime, I put some hydrogen peroxide around the nipple and areola, and then gauze over it in my bra. I needed to be careful.

Throughout the week, we talked about our marriage. Moments of disbelief still crept up, especially when he continued to call home. This seemed odd, considering the circumstances. Even though he didn't call from our room, his deceit was more unpalatable to me than ever.

He convinced me that in just a few more weeks, he would be mine, only mine, and I needed to trust him. I remembered what my boys had said to me—be patient and trusting. I tried my best to be both.

I was enthralled with his affection and words of love. He would kiss my tears away if I hurt. He was my gorgeous one. He was unstintingly generous with his wife-to-be. His insatiable appetite for me became contagious. I wanted more. We wanted each other relentlessly.

Eric made arrangements for us to take a hot-air balloon ride on Saturday morning. I had never done such a thing before, and the uniqueness of the adventure seemed an appropriate celebration of our new life. It fit into our love-affair fantasy.

The balloon rose over the earth and the Pacific shoreline and took the eight passenger high, then higher, away from all the concerns of everyday life. From the balloon, everything I had ever wanted from life seemed within reach.

As I squinted up into the balloon, its form looked like a striped, multicolored breast with a nipple in the center. At last I had found my rainbow.

My dream fell apart when we landed roughly. The balloon bounced on the ground several times, then tipped over. All seven people fell on top of me. I ducked in time not to get a bush in my face, but I landed on my new breast. I was shaken but okay.

Later that evening as I dressed for dinner, I realized my nipple had been injured. Some of the stitches had ripped open. I'd have Braun fix them when I got back to Sarasota. I worried about needing to have the entire surgical procedure redone.

We dined at a romantic, elegant oceanside restaurant, where we toasted to our celebration of life, then gazed out the window at the Pacific and talked about waves—that they have a shape that rises to a peak, then descends through a node that is at the same level as the waves' initiation. It is sent into a trough below the median, then it will rise again.

"It's like sex," Eric said, then smiled.

"Up and down, round and about, in and out."

We laughed at his comparison, then talked about how I was riding the crest of life, enjoying sublime happiness over my new soul mate and new breast.

I told him that I had to have a companion who was able to be a free spirit with me.

"We can see only part of a massive wave," I continued, "but we can feel the force that builds it. Isn't it the same universal energy that creates the spirit within our soul? The component we don't see is what gives us the strength and inspiration to live fully. A free spirit knows the other side of the wave—the hidden aspect—and can tap into the invisible energy."

We talked more about God. I still didn't completely understand my mission and purpose on Earth but hoped that when I was finished with my new book, it might provide an answer.

Saul called when I arrived home. We went for a

walk on the beach. I told him I had had a sensational trip to California, then explained the status of my relationship with Eric. Saul accepted that he and I would be friends and nothing more.

The next day, I went to see Braun. My nipple needed repair. It was a setback but, fortunately, nothing serious, and it wasn't painful. In fact, I experienced no pain throughout the entire reconstruction surgery and healing.

Three weeks later, Eric came down for a few days. His visit felt entirely different, now that he was definitely leaving home. We drove around and looked at real estate. He wanted a waterfront house on Siesta Key.

We saw an empty lot, parked the car, and strolled down to the shore. Next door, a man was carrying some potted plants onto a new terrace and dock. Eric walked over, introduced himself, and talked about looking for a house. The stranger said that he and his wife were considering putting their place on the market. He showed us around and introduced us to his wife. They said that was a second marriage for both of them and told us how happy they were. Eric told him we were planning what would be our second marriage.

The house was small but wonderful. Stained gray, it had one story, with a beautiful view, a white, newly remodeled kitchen, and a swimming pool outside the bedroom's french doors. A wonderful old tree stood just off the side of the pool deck. Eric pointed to it and said it could be my purple tree. He murmured that we could build a second floor after we got settled and started working.

The two men discussed finishing the dock with special provisions Eric wanted. They made arrangements to discuss price later, over the phone.

We got into the car, and I was almost too excited to sit still. We both wanted that house for our first love nest. All the happiness made our parting at the airport especially difficult.

As I drove home, I basked in the joy of his adoration and the belief that I would be loved, encouraged, and protected for the rest of my life. I tried to imagine living with a man who was wholly, unconditionally approving of me and whatever I chose to do. It would be wonderful to live in a supportive environment in our beautiful house by the water.

Eric sent me an extra check and a bouquet of long-stemmed purple roses. He called many times a day to say that he loved me. His thoughtfulness helped me endure the loneliness. I knew that if I sold my condo, he and I could manage well enough until he passed the board exams and got settled in his new career. The most important thing was that we'd be together. He told me that he would be retaining an attorney to initiate divorce proceedings.

My exhilaration interrupted my sleep. This year had been wonderful. He's leaving home. . . . He'll be here in two weeks. . . . I lay in bed, staring at the ceiling and hugging Eric's pillow. I buried my nose deeply in the down and tried to inhale his essence. I fantasized about the future, then got up and read *Journey*, to assure myself that the last nine years had actually happened.

The next evening I attended a concert of the Florida West Coast Symphony. A male friend came up and asked if I heard that a mutual acquaintance had died of breast cancer, which had spread rapidly throughout her body. I was shocked by the news. The woman had told me about her illness after she found out about *Journey* and I gave her a copy as a gift. Now she was gone. She had been my age. I felt sick and terrified by how fast life can change into death. My remission was a precious gift. Thank you, God, I thought, for giving me each day, the sun, my happiness.

I hurried home to call Ellie. She was home with her family and feeling better after another series of chemo. I told her about my upcoming marriage, and she and I rejoiced together. Maybe she will be able to dance at my wedding, after all.

CHAPTER 14

It was so much fun to walk nude around my house and watch my breasts move. I enjoyed wearing nothing under a blouse or shirt. I felt sexy, touching my round breasts and nipples. Braun may want the nipple to protrude a little more, or he may leave it alone.

I'm now the sum of all my parts. I'm whole. Complete.

Eric called many times a day, every day. He encouraged me to work on my new book and discussed his research with me as if I could understand it all.

When we were together, he would write with me. In bed or in my Jacuzzi, we discussed the manuscript. Often we made love before we finished talking, but he always laughed and said that we had a lifetime to complete our conversations.

I had put my condo on the market, but it hadn't sold. I considered lowering my asking price. My hope was to close on the place before Eric came down to study for his board exam. He had been helping me with extra money, and it felt right and good to know that soon I would be able to help him.

I decided to have a face-lift after my breasts were tattooed. Harsh lines had been etched around my mouth ever since my chemotherapy began, and they, too, were a constant reminder of troubled times. I decided to tell my boys of my plans and called them immediately after notifying Braun's office.

Marc and Joel found it difficult to relate to my physical and emotional changes. I love my sons, but our communications during the previous year had been strained. Now they immediately challenged me.

I told them about having my facial lines taken away.

"What the hell are you doing?" they demanded. "You're beautiful. What's going on with you?"

"I want cancer out of my face. I'm tired of looking at it every day."

I asked them simply to listen to my feelings and not to question them. I hung up the phone and wondered why I had to defend myself to everybody. I had seen Saul the night before, and although we enjoyed boating together, we were at loggerheads politically. I liked heated discussions about politics; he didn't. But Saul wasn't a priority in my life. I was too consumed with Eric, and a new concern had arisen: My beloved ex-father-in-law was very ill.

Dad Chechik was a great friend and father to me. We were together since the middle 1950s.

He was my strength when my life was difficult after divorcing his son. Also, Dad was my anchor of love and courage throughout my cancer fight. Dad Chechik was a general in my army of supporters.

Dad Chechik and his wife lived in St. Petersburg, about an hour north of Sarasota. During my boys' last visit, we all went to see him in a nursing home. That afternoon, Dad showed a few precious moments of clarity. I had stayed behind and hugged him after everyone else had left. He looked at me and put his hand on my face.

"Diane," he said, "I might not remember too much of our lives, but I do know I love you very much. Keep your smile and stay healthy. I'm sorry I can't help you more."

I kissed him and said that I had loved him all of my adult life. He was a wonderful father. We hugged again. The affectionate bond we built had never faltered. Some people thought I had married my husband because his dad was so terrific.

While other family members went biking or hiking, Dad and I would talk alone for hours about feelings and his business ideas. He had been my best friend for thirty-six years. Now, he was dying. I made arrangements to visit him in the nursing home the next morning. In the afternoon, my friends Winona and Rolf would be arriving from Madison, and I had invited them to stay at my house.

Three days after my visit to St. Petersburg, I answered a call from Eric.

"I left," he said.

"You left what?" I asked.

"I left home. I'm flying down to pick you up. You're coming back to Madison with me."

"You've told her?" My voice shook.

"Yes, her, the kids, and anyone else who would listen." He sounded ecstatic and proud of himself. "I'll call you at two o'clock from St. Louis, just before I get on the connecting flight. Pick me up at three-thirty in Sarasota." He hung up.

I screamed with disbelief and began jumping up and down. Winona hurried into my living room to see if I was all right. I hugged her, then danced around the room. Rolf came in and when he learned what was happening asked if I would like him and Winona to get a room in a motel so we could be alone.

I told him no, that I'd be going back to Madison with Eric and, in fact, would appreciate their house-sitting for me until I returned.

When I stopped shaking, I called the boys, Aunt Nish and Uncle George, and Gladys and Milt.

I couldn't believe this was finally, actually happening. Eric taking the jump. He had become one of the privileged few.

He called again at two, just to say how much he loved me and that he was looking forward to our life together. I was soaring.

We were aware the road ahead would present difficulties, but he wanted me to be at his side for them. We would support each other. We'd live together in Madison in the summer and fall, and he'd commute to Sarasota during the winter while I stayed in Florida.

I told him I'd see him at the airport at three thirty. The next ninety minutes could not have passed quickly enough to suit me. I got to the airport early, parked, then paced the long concourse outside his gate while I waited for his plane to land.

When he arrived, he looked strangely disheartened.

"Eric! What's wrong?"

He kissed me, then guided me to an empty bank of chairs in the waiting area. "I called her from St. Louis," he said with a grimace. "She's agreed to go into counseling."

My heart sank.

"I told her I'd go with her. It's the proper thing to do. It might help free me."

I sat frozen.

"Would you be willing to wait for a week?" he implored. "I'll be back. You can fly home with me then."

I was in shock. I didn't want to give him an answer. "L-Let's think about it," I finally managed to say. "It might be better if I were with you next week."

An air of celebration had always marked our rides from the airport to Siesta Key, with much talking, laughing, interrupting, and touching; but this time we were uncharacteristically somber. He was aware that Winona and Rolf were at my condo. Instead of going home, we ran to the beach, held hands, kissed, and prayed together. Then we went home to get him unpacked and settled.

We talked with Winona and Rolf, and Eric professed his love for me and his sadness about having to fulfill his obligation. The Ruehls were understanding, said all the right things, then made themselves scarce. We retreated to the bedroom and made love. It held an undercurrent of desperation. We couldn't stop clinging to each other.

Afterwards, we got dressed, and he called his daughter and sister. I talked with both of them. He told them that I was the most important love of his life. I listened and felt disassociated, as if this were a dream. But for the moment, it was real enough.

Next he called the owners of the gray house on the

bay and asked if we could drop by for a few minutes. They said yes, and we drove right over. We walked through the place, which was just as wonderful as we had remembered it, then sat on the bench built into the terrace on the deck. We held hands and watched silently as the bay waters moved out with the tide.

We ultimately decided that he had to go back alone. He would return to me the next weekend. We made a pact that I would be in Wisconsin for one week, then return to Florida. Meanwhile, he would look for a place for us to live in Madison.

The morning before he left, Eric officially became a Floridian. He used my address as his permanent residency and gave up his residency in Wisconsin. He got his voter's registration card. In six months, he could obtain a Florida divorce. Meanwhile, he would study for his boards.

As he got on the plane, he promised he would never give me up, no matter what it would take for us to be together.

PART THREE
CHAPTER 15

It was over. Yesterday was gone. So was Eric.

He went back to his wife. Just twenty-four hours before, he was talking about our being married. He was going to see his attorney. Maybe he had seen him and found out how much the divorce was going to cost. He might not want to sacrifice his money. Maybe he already had a new woman—the divorced physician he had casually mentioned to me. Maybe if I had gone to Madison with him yesterday, things would have turned out differently. Maybe his so-called intentions to leave were his way to end our relationship. What made me think he wouldn't do the same thing to me as he had done to his wife?

The marital therapist told him that he could neither talk to me nor see me for six weeks. Eric agreed to those restrictions before asking me how I would feel about them. He hadn't been strong enough to prevail against the wishes of the therapist. He hadn't protected me during this decision. He protected himself. The truth was if he really meant to leave, he would have left. Eric Meyer does everything he wants to do. But I found it impossible to believe that after all of his loving, he could have given me up so completely and so abruptly.

I could have kicked myself for suggesting that he go into counseling! I was wrong. He and I could have made it together. I wasn't the cause of his marital problems. He might have implied to the therapist that I ran after him. I was so angry at myself, even though I knew, in my heart, this probably would happen to me. I was hurting.

Eric's last words before I hung up the phone were, "I love you. I went after you the first time, and the second time I will catch you."

I told him not to be so sure.

He said, "I'm sure, Diane."

I felt as if my heart had been ripped out of my chest. I felt humiliated in front of my family and friends and even my doctors. I felt like a fool.

After a sleepless night, I called Saul and told him that I'd like to see him for dinner. He was delighted. I went over to his house and cried. I told him the truth about Eric.

Saul held me as I wept. "He probably didn't intend to fall in love with you," he consoled. "Probably he just wanted to have some fun and got in over his head."

I was so distraught, Saul was afraid for me to be

alone. He invited me to stay at his place and offered to sleep in the guest room. I accepted. I didn't want to be alone. My love was gone.

He tucked me in and kissed me good-night. I looked around, disoriented. What am I doing in a stranger's bed? I wondered through a veil of tears. What's happening to my life?

I suffered through a long, painful night. I cried as Eric's and my fantasies of the past two years replayed before my eyes. I knew he wouldn't come back, and I tried to convince myself that never seeing him again would be the best thing for me, in spite of my anguish.

Further realities of my situation sank in. I'd have to call the couple with whom he was negotiating for the house and tell them that the deal is off. And without his aid my finances were a mess. What was I going to do?

I observed the one-year anniversary of my reconstruction surgery by having my tattoo. And yet, the depth of my grief was so great, I couldn't take pleasure even in that.

I missed Eric terribly every aching moment of the day. I honored his request not to call him, but whenever I walked the beach, I hallucinated his running toward me, arms outstretched in love. Although I was strong enough not to call again, I privately whispered to him on my beach.

Exhausted, I prayed I wouldn't get sick. I was worried about stress, and that created a vicious circle. I believe anxiety causes cancer by depressing the immune system. I sat under my purple tree more often. I needed to gather all my strength so I wouldn't falter. My destiny, I reminded myself, is based on my ability to change my life.

I tried but found it impossible to believe that a man who wrote me love poems would never speak to me again.

For two nights in a row, the phone rang, but when I picked it up, the party at the other end, without uttering a word, hung up. I knew the calls probably were Eric's.

At times my anger overrode my grief. I was infuriated that he hadn't considered what would happen to me as a result of this estrangement. He had done this all on his own, without discussion. He hadn't taken my health or my feelings into consideration. I would not have agreed to six weeks without communication.

We were not guilty of any "crime" except falling in love. I was his salvation and showed him another way of life. Who was the real Eric? I wondered, but couldn't find an answer.

As my anger grew, so did my resolve. I decided not to be his victim, any more than I had been a victim of cancer. I needed to get rid of him, exactly as I had ridded myself of my cancer. The process, I guessed, would be similar to a year of chemotherapy, killing off the cells of love.

I vowed never again to have anything to do with a married man. He was the first and last.

Saul was very kind and understanding, but he was not Eric. We went on a boat ride, then cooked dinner together. He wanted to make love, but I was grieving. I couldn't—not then.

I urgently wanted Saul to be my new love. I wanted him to slide neatly into the void left by Eric and say to me, "Diane, I will be everything you want and more. I will love and take care of you." But Saul, as wonderful as he had been to me, was still Saul. He was extremely judgmental about everything and everyone—a most glaring contrast to Eric, who was unreservedly accepting and encouraging. How I had enjoyed and appreciated that!

Miserable, I decided to call my dear pal Ellie for solace. I learned she was back in the hospital for more chemo, so I phoned her there. When I heard her sick voice, I knew I couldn't burden her with my problems. She tried to sound upbeat and said she was planning to go on her "dream trip" with her husband to Australia and New Zealand. They were hoping to leave in a few weeks.

I told her I was thrilled for her, but I did not feel optimistic when I hung up the receiver. Oh, God, I thought, don't take Ellie from me, too.

CHAPTER 16

Three Months Later

This was the first morning I had walked the beach since my face surgery—another great decision. The sun rose large and red as I walked the crystal sands—a perfect morning in paradise.

Most of my lines of stress from the last ten years had been erased with my face-lift. I looked as if I'd had a great night's sleep. Not only were my cancer stress lines gone, the scars from my reconstruction had faded.

As I walked, a vision of my former father-in-law appeared before me. I knew that Dad was scheduled that day to have his leg amputated up to his thigh. An infection due to his circulation problem had grown severe. I could hear him crying and telling me that he would not live with the indignity the amputation would impose.

I hurried home and dialed his son's phone number for the first time in thirteen years, violating the court order that prohibited us from contacting each other. I told his secretary that I did not wish to identify myself. She put me through, and he answered.

"This is Diane," I told him.

At first his voice was low and very sexy.

I said, "This is Diane Craig Chechik."

"Oh, hello," he said coldly.

I told him the reason for my call was to urge him to come down immediately if he wanted to see his dad alive. I implored him to stop the surgery until he had consulted with the University of Wisconsin Infectious Disease Department or the Center for Disease Control in Atlanta.

"Don't let them amputate Dad's leg," I begged. "Please. He'll die."

"There's no reason to get so upset," he told me angrily. "This is a routine operation."

I felt outraged by his reply concerning Dad. My voice had a tone of both sadness and horror as I said, "Cutting off a body part is never routine. Take his age into consideration." I hadn't wanted to tell him about my vision, but I was getting nowhere and was horribly distressed. "He's going to die. I know it."

"Good-bye, Diane," he said, and hung up.

The next day, while my ex-husband was attending a business meeting in Green Bay, Wisconsin, his father, Samuel R. Chechik, passed away.

I took pleasure in Saul, and he made my loss easier to bear. His affection for me seemed genuine. When we eventually became lovers, he was astonished by my surgery.

He wanted to have an exclusive relationship with me, but I knew that wasn't possible—not after what had happened with me and Eric. Furthermore, he couldn't give me what I really wanted. I had decided that relationships needed to keep moving and to go someplace.

I spent a significant amount of time alone, to grieve and think and learn as many lessons as possible from my misery. My decision to see my problems as challenges and to benefit from their lessons gave me strength and confidence.

A friend once suggested that problems were simply opportunities for personal growth. God, I've had some terrific opportunities! I conjured up my purple tree whenever I needed to feel safe. I watched branches of courage, strength, and love sprout new leaves. Most often this happened on the beach, where I could listen to the surf and watch the dolphins. The gulf was my holy water; the shoreline was my place for spiritual growth.

The sandpipers and egrets patrolled the shoreline. Inevitably one bird would be flying in the opposite direction from the flock or standing alone. That one reminded me of myself. By moving forward, by abandoning the past, I had changed. I had made new footsteps in my path.

I learned that we have every option available when choosing our way of life. A person can change her life and make the choice to be empowered, or lag behind and remain imprisoned by fear, low self-esteem, or, as in my case, breast cancer. I chose empowerment, survival, health, and freedom. My change had to come unless I wanted to be consumed by more cancer.

Filled with new positive energy and inner peace, I believed I was the luckiest woman in the world. I'm a damned miracle! I assured myself. I want someone who says that our relationship is a miracle.

I learned that I would never be an enabler again because that is ultimately self-destructive. I vowed to do only what was positive for me in my new life.

I learned that having cancer can be empowering if you survive. Your perspective shifts. There's no way you can fight like hell and endure the pain without its having an effect on you. Victory over cancer is a private war, which loved ones may never understand. A successful battle can serve as an inspiration to struggle against anything else in the world that causes you pain. When I moved to Sarasota, I began to give away my pain. I found myself and my paradise there.

I learned that anyone who doesn't have a vision can't have a place to go. She cannot be empowered because she has no vision to move her to a new realm. Already I was moving on to something greater, although I did not have a clear picture of what that new goal might be. My vision, my dream, my power, my breasts, all are a part of my life. I take none of them for granted. I worked hard for my precious gift of life.

I could feel my heart beating faster as I approached Dr. Isaac Levine's office for my semiannual checkup. This was the first time I drove by myself to Naples. I wanted my freedom. After the examination, Isaac, his wife, and I were going to have lunch together.

Several days before, I had had a mammogram and chest X ray taken at Radiology Associates in Sarasota. Isaac wanted to read the films and written report from the radiologist, and I arranged to drive the packet to Naples.

After I had the X ray, instead of waiting the customary three days for the results, I had the good news within hours by asking Braun's office to call the radiologist for me. Everything was fine. I felt very relieved.

When Isaac came into the examining room, he gave me a big hug. He remarked that I looked rested, and my face looked aglow. Then his tone became quiet. "Your loss of Eric is more his loss," Isaac said. "His aliveness hinged upon being with you. Your aliveness is with yourself."

I thanked him for his kindness.

"I heard an expression I'd like to pass along to

you," he continued. "'A man or woman goes through life either parking their car or driving their car.' You're driving through life, Diane. Eric is at a standstill."

After my appointment, we went to the restaurant. As we were about to order, Isaac's beeper called him to an emergency. He said a quick good-bye and was gone.

The word *emergency* rang in my ears and shook me to my marrow. The word, I thought, characterized my past life. In retrospect I realized that I had lived in a state of medical crisis for almost eight years. Because cancer cells multiply with horrific speed, devouring all the good cells and eventually killing the patient, I was constantly aware of the possibility of dying. The feelings of danger and uncertainty gave my day-to-day existence a sense of urgency. I wondered how long Isaac's patient's life had been an emergency and when and how the emergency would be resolved.

I took some deep, calming breaths and wiped my clammy hands on my napkin. We would have many lunches together in our future, I reminded myself. I'm on medical alert no more.

CHAPTER 17

Nine Months Later

It was freezing outside, but our family love warmed the inside of Joel and Sara's house in Minneapolis. Marc and his girlfriend came in from St. Louis for the holidays. They looked extremely happy in each other's company. Sara's parents and her sister's family joined us. There was love all around.

Joel helped me prepare my seafood bisque, which has been our traditional Christmas Eve supper. While we cooked, he told me that I ought to think about finding a new challenge.

The boys handed me a flat, rectangular present. When I tore off the wrapping paper, I found a beautiful beach scene that Dad Chechik had drawn while he was living in the nursing home. The boys had had it framed for me. I stared at the gift and felt overwhelmed. My father-in-law and I had shared a love for the beach and the water, and he had captured that emotion in his drawing.

My boys' understanding of Dad's and my closeness touched me deeply. They could not have given me a more precious gift. I burst into tears and ran into my room, where I sobbed uncontrollably. I knew that I was crying for those whom I missed so terribly and were with me only in spirit—my mother, my father, Dad Chechik, countless friends, and, of course, Eric, who was alive and well, I presumed, but unreachable.

When my tears stopped, I washed my face and repaired my makeup, to make myself presentable for the Christmas Eve service at the Unitarian church. I looked forward to being in church that night; I wanted to give thanks. God had given me His blessing, manifested in my health.

Finally I opened the bedroom door, and Joel and Marc were waiting for me in the hallway, leaning against the wall. Concern tightened their features. They both wrapped their arms around me and said, "We love you, Mom."

Sara came upstairs, and she offered her help and love. She wanted to know if she could do anything to make me feel better.

I took the opportunity to say what needed to be expressed for a long, long time. I told Joel, Sara, and Marc that I had to be honest and real with them. I had to be free to be myself and pursue my own agenda. I explained that I had been through some arduous years and was still rebalancing my emotional and physical life. I wanted their love and support.

My adoring family heard my words and tenderly enveloped me in a family hug. Now I was shedding tears of joy.

I received my first call in a year from Eric. In a flat, controlled voice, he told me that Ellie had died. She had pulled out all her tubes and chosen to live without medication for the last days of her life. He knew I would be extremely saddened, maybe even frightened, and would want to make a donation in her memory to the University of Wisconsin Cancer Clinic. He was going to send a condolence note to her family.

I was shocked by the news and was also off balance from hearing his voice again after all the long, lonely months. I wanted to get off the phone and cry for Ellie. But at the same time I wanted to keep him talking, so I could take pleasure and pain in the sound of his dear and hated voice. I wanted to know everything that was going on in his life, and yet I wanted to know nothing. I sat numb and silent, the receiver to my ear.

He said that he had had enough of our year of silence. I asked him outright if he was seeing another woman.

He hesitated, then answered, "Yes. I started seeing

her shortly after our . . . parting. I had to have someone if I couldn't have you."

I felt disgust. Those might have been the most honest words he had ever spoken to me.

"How did you know I was involved with someone?" he asked.

"Simple—you couldn't go through this alone."

I told him I had finished my book and was working on the revisions with Laurie Rosin. He was proud of me for having accomplished so much during our year apart. Then his voice took on a softer tone, and he said, "I love you, Diane. I hope we will always be friends."

Without answering I said good-bye and ended the call. I sat paralyzed, trying to make sense of it all. Maybe he cared for me enough to spare me from pain of his activities. Or perhaps, he actually believed in his love for me and the life he and I shared. He might have thought that he could change . . . until the last moment. But whatever the reasons for his leaving me, it all had been just make-believe.

I hadn't seen Saul for months. I considered calling him because he wouldn't be my rebound anymore—I had finally gotten over yearning for Eric. But something stopped me from making that call.

Then, in February, Saul and I bumped into each other at the Arts Day Festival. I was glad to see him. We both were alone, and he invited me out for a cup of coffee. We went to a small cafe and talked about how we were feeling.

Our conversation was very relaxed. I had mentally released him from my unrealistic expectations of filling Eric's shoes. I was able to enjoy Saul for who he was. After about an hour, I had to leave for dinner with a girlfriend. He walked me to my car.

"Saul," I said, "I'm sorry about our past. I got rid of ghosts. I'm different now."

"But you still look beautiful," he told me. "You usually do." He bent down and kissed me. "I could have been more gentle with you," he admitted. "Not so judgmental."

He told me he would call, and I replied that I'd look forward to hearing from him. This was the first step in building a new life for myself. I felt better for having taken it.

EPILOGUE

I feel the warmth and protection of my purple tree. I'm closer to heaven here, my safe place to dream and live. I close my eyes and see a forest of purple trees. I'm committed to being well.

Sometimes I'm terrified of the unknown. But as Georgia O'Keeffe once said, "I might be terrified, but I won't let that stand in the way of my living."

When I made the decision to have reconstructive surgery, I believed I had a future. My attitude enabled me to leave behind my cancer-victim identity and look forward to a long and happy life. The concept of wellness convinced me that I had more than just the pleasures of the day.

As my two new breasts created a balance between my bodyself and my feelings, I enjoyed a new calm and confidence.

Healthy breasts are symbols of our femininity and motherhood. I wrote this journal for everyone who wants to acknowledge the importance of her womanhood surviving a battle with breast cancer. Isn't our sexuality essential to our life? Aren't men part of our hunt?

My life is my success. My ultimate victory is that I have outlived Dr. Bob Jackson, who died suddenly at the age of sixty-six.

My empowerment is a celebration of my new world. I'm all together. I'm an extraordinarily fortunate woman. I spread my arms to embrace my life with enormous vigor and great expectations.

My purple tree still gives me strength and the dreams and visions for planting. Even now, I look up and watch new branches and tender, sparkling leaves cover the crown of my tree. Some branches are sturdier, darker, and more mature than others. Some are feathery, with room to grow. Their shades of purple have changed with me.

I have no limits when I'm sitting under my tree. My spirit lives eternally. I will not falter. What I accomplished during my cancer life matters, but even more important, my new identity is flourishing. My mission is not over. Maybe that's why I'm alive!

Wellness will come to those who fight for it and are blessed with luck, and love will be there for those who risk to open their heart.

Hurray for my recognizing my moment of truth. I know, truly, there's nothing like a breast!

Though my diary, *There's Nothing Like a Breast,* is complete, each day I continue to fight my own personal, cancer war; it's never-ending.

The two tablets of Tamoxifen® I take each day are my ammunition. I have taken them for the past sixteen years. I will take them for the rest of my life.

I receive strength and courage sitting under my purple tree. It exists always—whenever and wherever I need it. I am in touch with my emotions and sexuality. They evolve and grow proportionately and positively—as my self-esteem and self-image of being a breast cancer survivor grow.

I hope through my diary I have been able to give you new perspectives—ammunition, if you will—for fighting your battle. As you live and fight each day, I wish you good health.

Diane

<u>YOUR NOTES</u>

YOUR NOTES

YOUR NOTES